WAY

ALLEN COUNTY PUBLIC LIBRARY

3 1833 02520 4378

005.43 W72ch
Christian, Kaare, 1954-
How Windows works

P9-ECX-892

DO N   /E
CARDS   CKET

HOW WINDOWS WORKS

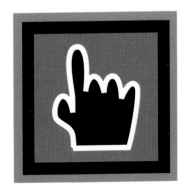

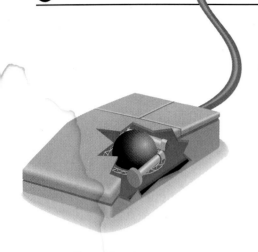

Introduction xi

PART 1

Windows and DOS
1

Chapter 1
How Windows and DOS
Are Organized..........................4

Chapter 2
How Windows and DOS
Use Memory 8

Chapter 3
How Windows Boots 14

PART 2

The Graphical Interface
21

Chapter 4
How the Display Works 24

Chapter 5
How the User Interface
Works 32

Chapter 6
How Dialog Boxes Work 42

Chapter 7
How Drawing Works 48

Chapter 8
How Fonts and Typefaces
Work 56

Chapter 9
How Cursors and Icons
Work 64

PART 3

The Built-In Windows Utilities
71

Chapter 10
How Program Manager
Works 74

Chapter 11
How File Manager Works 80

Chapter 12
How the Control Panel
Works 86

Chapter 13
How Windows Help
Works 92

PART 4

Application to Application
99

Chapter 14
How the Clipboard
Works......................................102

Chapter 15
How Dynamic Data Exchange
Works......................................108

Chapter 16
How Object Linking and
Embedding Works 114

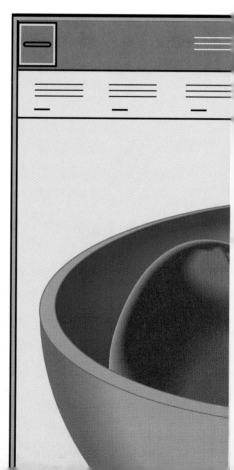

PART 5
The Multimedia Experience
121

PART 6
Behind the Scenes
143

PART 7
Running Applications
173

Chapter 17
How Windows Makes Sounds 124

Chapter 18
How Windows Plays Video Clips 130

Chapter 19
How Animation Works........136

Chapter 20
How Messages Work 146

Chapter 21
How DLLs Work 152

Chapter 22
How Virtual Memory Works.....................................158

Chapter 23
How Input and Output Device Drivers Work 164

Chapter 24
How Windows Runs Windows Applications...........................176

Chapter 25
How Windows Runs DOS Applications...........................182

Chapter 26
How Multitasking Works.....188

Index 194

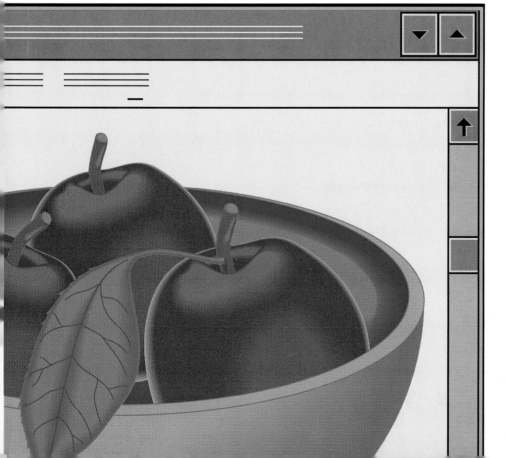
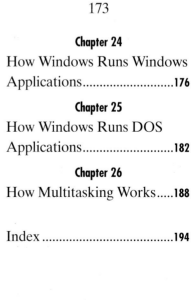

Without the lively, colorful, and engaging work of artist Pamela Drury Wattenmaker, this book would be sadly diminished. Pamela conceived of the androids that populate most drawings; she worked hard to add visual interest to all of the drawings, and she often enhanced my ideas to make the drawings clearer and more informative. Even more important to me, she could take my sketches (though the word *sketches* denotes far too much) and return elegant and finished drawings. Thanks, Pamela!

Many people at ZD Press contributed to this book, although Melinda Levine and Cindy Hudson are the two I worked with the most. Cindy convinced me to do the book; both Cindy and Melinda were involved in the early stages of concept and outline; and then Melinda worked with me on it through to the finish. I'm grateful to both of them for their helpful comments and criticisms.

My principal research tool for this book was the Microsoft Developer Network CD, which is a CD-ROM reference containing virtually everything published by Microsoft about Windows. As I used Windows to prepare my manuscript, I was able to display my text in one window, my reference materials in another, and the current drawing in a third. (And please don't fault me for using a developer's reference to write a book for people who aren't developers. First and foremost, I wanted to get it right, so I went to the source.)

I'm very thankful that my family supported me throughout this work. My children learned to wait for homework help until they saw my attention wander from the screen, and my wife indulged my long hours and occasional bad temper. Thanks for the understanding, Kari, Arli, Reed, and Robin.

Kaare Christian
New York City

The desktop computer revolution is fueled by a huge range of technology breakthroughs, from basic physics of atoms and molecules, to the esoteric realms of automata theory, linguistics, and programming heuristics. In between these breakthroughs lies the signature marvel of the late twentieth century—the chip, the no-less-amazing miracle of mass storage technology, and a revolution in networking and other forms of communication that has profoundly changed how we live and work.

The enormous range of technology that powers the desktop computer makes it hard to answer the seemingly simple question: "How does Windows work?" The answer could wander into physics, chemistry, chip design, computer architecture, or a half dozen other esoteric topics. But I think the most interesting and informative way to answer the question is to focus on software, because it's software that gives the personal computer its personality.

But even narrowing the answer to the field of software still leaves a very broad subject! Software itself ranges from the primitive BIOS software that's built into every PC to provide rudimentary operations, to state-of-the-art Windows applications such as WordPerfect for Windows or CorelDRAW. But the personality of a Windows PC is primarily resident in Windows itself, which is why I decided to focus only on Windows.

So that all Windows users, not just software developers, could enjoy this book, I decided to look at Windows from a user's perspective. But even though my tour is from a user's point of view, many features of Windows normally seen by only software developers, such as software messages and dynamic link libraries, are on display for your enjoyment.

What I expect from you is a working knowledge of Windows. If you can start Windows, open an application, get something accomplished, and then save your work, you know enough about Windows to enjoy this book.

This book primarily covers Windows 3.1. At the time of writing, 3.1 is by far the predominant version of Windows. This book also applies to Windows for Workgroups, because the core of that product is the same as Windows 3.1, although I don't discuss any of Windows for Workgroup's networking extensions. Much of this book also applies to Windows NT and to future desktop Windows systems.

As the book progresses, there's a gradual shift in emphasis from aspects of Windows that you can see to aspects that are hidden inside. The visible and the hidden parts of Windows are equally important, although sometimes the hidden parts are harder to explain. Feel free to read the book in any order, because there are cross-references when necessary to guide you to supporting chapters.

WINDOWS AND DOS

CONTENTS

Chapter 1: How Windows and DOS Are Organized
4

Chapter 2: How Windows and DOS Use Memory
8

Chapter 3: How Windows Boots
14

WINDOWS GIVES LIFE to modern PCs; it's what sets new PCs apart from their dull, typewriterlike forebears. Windows gives you a graphical environment, so you can see what you're doing. Windows gives you a consistent point-and-shoot user interface, so that all your software works alike. And Windows gives you the ability to run multiple programs at once, so your computer can keep up with the most valuable resource around—you.

Windows is now the undisputed champion of desktop computing. It's the environment that everyone is using, and that every software company is targeting for future development. However, though Windows is the champ now, just a couple years back, the desktop champion was DOS, Microsoft's venerable disk operating system. DOS hasn't been completely evicted from your machine: When your computer is first turned on, it still boots to DOS. Surprisingly, DOS has remained relatively unchanged since 1983. Yes, nearly unchanged even as PC hardware has doubled in performance and capability every two to three years.

In a nutshell, Windows 3.1 turbocharges DOS. It adds a racy, high-performance superstructure to DOS's modest frame. Windows is like a Formula One racecar that has been built atop a motor-scooter chassis. While the racecar is roaring around the track, it's not obvious that there's a scooter inside. But to really understand the racecar, you need to look at how its sleek chassis has been bolted onto the wobbly motor-scooter frame.

The chapters in this part explore how Windows and DOS work together. Chapter 1 presents a software organization chart, which shows how the two systems are organized. In the DOS world, applications create their own user interface, and they often work directly with hardware, especially with printers and the display. And it's one application at a time in DOS. The Windows system is organized differently, with Windows taking responsibility for many more services. This means all applications can work alike, and all applications can concentrate on a given task, rather than on printer support and other tedious chores. And Windows is a communal, communicative place, with more going on at once. Much more fun!

Memory is the coin in modern computing, so Chapter 2 looks at how DOS and Windows use memory. The legendary 640K barrier is one of DOS's greatest liabilities; breaking it was one of Windows's greatest triumphs. This may sound academic, but it has profound consequences. Better use of memory is the key to sound, video, graphics, multitasking, and all the other sophisticated, engaging features of Windows.

Chapter 3 shows how you can get there (Windows) from here (DOS). When your PC first gets power, it loads DOS. From DOS, the road to Windows is long and winding, but intriguing to watch and satisfying to understand. By the end of the process, Windows has constructed itself from its components, it has taken the reins of your hardware, making full use of your CPU and memory, and it has started a desktop manager, usually Windows's own Program Manager.

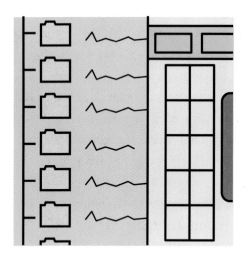

How Windows and DOS Are Organized

A DECADE AGO, DOS seemed like a marvel. It brought computing to the desktop, created an industry, made fortunes for a few, and changed the face of business throughout the world. All this from a little software package that really doesn't do very much. All DOS provides is a simple system for storing files, a way to launch programs, and a very thin software shield that separates applications from the hardware.

DOS was a nice solid system for the early eighties, but it doesn't provide nineties services. It lacks user-interface components such as menus; it provides only the simplest printing services; its video display driver is primitive and rarely used; and DOS doesn't know about sound or graphics. When needed, DOS applications have to provide these components for themselves. Even worse, DOS limits the party to one application at a time.

These limitations of DOS can be seen on the left page of the accompanying illustration. Like the DOS spreadsheet shown in the figure, many DOS applications make little use of color or graphics. Because DOS provides so little, DOS applications must be self-sufficient. Like settlers on the frontier building their own shelter and providing their own sustenance, DOS applications must supply their own basic services.

Windows has a richer structure than DOS does, as shown on the right page of the accompanying illustration. Windows's applications are both graphical and colorful. This is easy for Windows programs, because Windows contains standard graphics drivers for both the screen and the printer, so that applications themselves don't need to tend to the details. Plus Windows contains user-interface components, such as menus, buttons, and dialog boxes, so that applications work alike. And best of all, Windows can coordinate multiple tasks at once, so you can view and work with several applications simultaneously—up to six or eight can be active at once. This richer, more organized environment comes from Windows's improved use of memory. That's why there is room for better drivers, for rich user-interface (UI) components, and even for several applications to be active simultaneously.

Windows's set of services lets programs concentrate on their chosen task. Word processors can process words; spreadsheets can concentrate on numbers; databases can concentrate on data. And because Windows lets programs communicate with each other, it's easy to share data. But perhaps most importantly, you can concentrate on getting your own work done, because all Windows applications work alike.

How Windows and DOS Are Organized

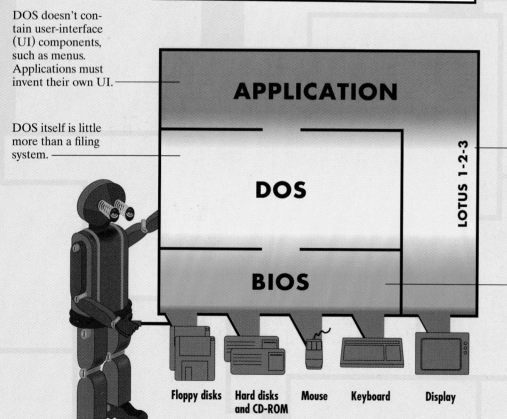

Worksheet Range Copy Move File Print				MENU
	A	B	C	D
1				
2				
3	Income	Salary	$13,090	
4		Tips	25,392	
5		Gifts	5,000	
6				
7		Total	$43,482	
8				
9	Expenses	Rent	$ 6,000	
10		Phone	2,400	
11		IRA	2,000	
12		E-Mail	700	

DOS doesn't contain user-interface (UI) components, such as menus. Applications must invent their own UI.

DOS itself is little more than a filing system.

APPLICATION

DOS

BIOS

LOTUS 1-2-3

Most applications use their own video driver and printer driver, as shown here, although some use the BIOS's primitive video driver.

The BIOS—which stands for *basic input/output system*—is software that is stored permanently in the computer. It contains device drivers for all the standard input/output devices, such as disks, keyboard, and display.

Floppy disks **Hard disks and CD-ROM** **Mouse** **Keyboard** **Display**

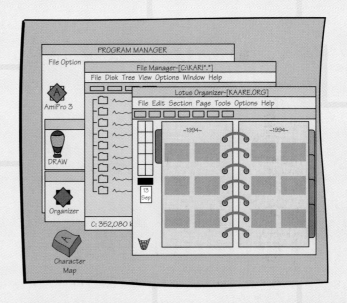

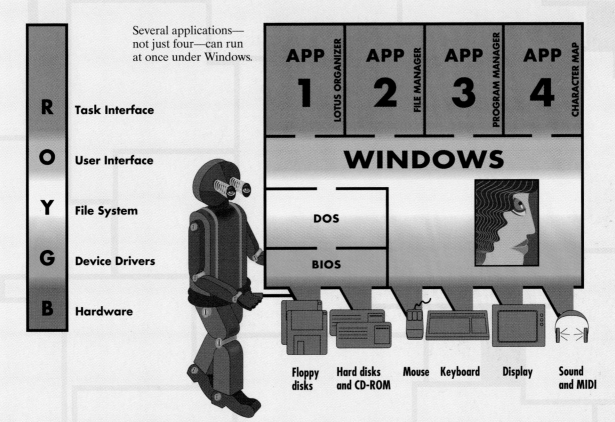

Several applications—
not just four—can run
at once under Windows.

R — Task Interface

O — User Interface

Y — File System

G — Device Drivers

B — Hardware

APP **1** LOTUS ORGANIZER

APP **2** FILE MANAGER

APP **3** PROGRAM MANAGER

APP **4** CHARACTER MAP

WINDOWS

DOS

BIOS

Floppy disks   Hard disks and CD-ROM   Mouse   Keyboard   Display   Sound and MIDI

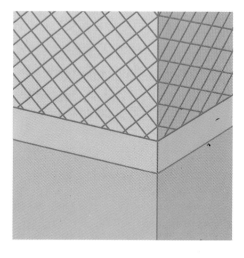

How Windows and DOS Use Memory

IF YOUR MACHINE was purchased in the last few years, chances are that it has two, four, eight, or more megabytes of memory. What is a megabyte? Well, a *byte* is a chunk of memory big enough to hold a small number (between 0 and 255), or a single keyboard character. If you have bigger numbers or whole words, then you need several bytes of memory. A *megabyte*? That's just a million bytes, all lined up in a row. But let's be more descriptive. A megabyte of memory can store about 300 single-spaced typewritten pages, or it can store a single full-page black-and-white image at laser-printer resolution, or it is about a quarter of the minimum necessary to run a graphical environment such as Windows.

If you're operating your PC with DOS, then you're running at half throttle, because DOS itself can manage only a tad more than half a megabyte. To be precise, DOS can manage 640 kilobytes (640K) of memory (1K is 1,024 bytes of memory; 640K is just over half a megabyte). That's because DOS was built for the original IBM PC, which was first delivered with 64K of memory, but could be expanded to 256K. Heady days!

The left page of the accompanying illustration details the history of memory usage on PCs. The original IBM PC was based on the Intel 8088 central processing unit (CPU). A computer's CPU—commonly called the brain—is the place where all the arithmetic and decision making occurs.

PCs that use an 8088 CPU have the memory organization shown in the left side of the figure. The Intel 8088 CPU could potentially work with 1 megabyte of memory. But IBM reserved a large chunk of the 8088's memory space for special purposes, leaving just over half for memory.

Subsequent PCs from IBM and other companies were based on later Intel CPUs, starting with the 286, and continuing with the 386, 486, and today's Pentium CPU. All of these CPUs retain compatibility with the 8088 because of the huge library of software written for the early PC. These improved Intel CPUs follow exactly the floorplan of the original 8088 CPU.

The right page of the accompanying figure shows how DOS and Windows use the memory on modern (post-8088) PCs. When DOS is in control, you can see that DOS and DOS applications are jammed into the first megabyte, even while memory above 1 megabyte is unused. There are a few specialized DOS device drivers, such as the VDISK virtual disk driver, that can make some use of the memory above 1 megabyte, but this is a weak and limited approach. When Windows is in control, all of the memory in the PC can be used. Let's see just how this works.

If a hotel has only rooms with single-digit room numbers, then it can reserve just ten rooms for its guests, rooms 0 through 9. But if the hotel uses two-digit room numbers, the number of possible rooms climbs to 100, rooms 0 through 99. Computer CPUs follow the same principle, although a few details are different. The most important difference is that computers work with base two (binary) numbers, in which each digit is either 0 or 1. Base two is used for computers, because 1s and 0s (on and off) are the natural system for digital electronics. Later CPUs such as the 486, which is used in many of today's Windows PCs, has additional binary digits (bits) for accessing memory that gives them the potential to muscle past the memory limitations of an 8088-based PC.

But is that potential used? Under DOS, it's not, because DOS doesn't unlock these additional bits for accessing memory. Windows starts fresh, with the clear intention of using all your PC has to offer, from the full memory space to sound and video. Windows unlocks the additional memory space by instructing the CPU chips to use their full memory-addressing capability. This lets Windows run several applications at once, play sound chips, show graphics, and do many other tasks that rely on access to megabytes of memory.

3 1833 02520 4378

How Windows and DOS Use Memory

Subsequent (80286 and higher) PC Memory Architecture

Newer Intel CPUs can use either 24- or 32-digit binary numbers to specify memory locations. The extra 4 or 12 binary digits allow the CPU to access memory above 1 megabyte.

The full memory space is usually partly unoccupied.

The room for additional memory varies. On a 286 or 386SX CPU, it's 15 megabytes; on a 386 or higher CPU, it's 4,095 megabytes.

For compatibility, newer Intel CPUs can also use the 8088's 20-digit addressing mode, which is called real mode.

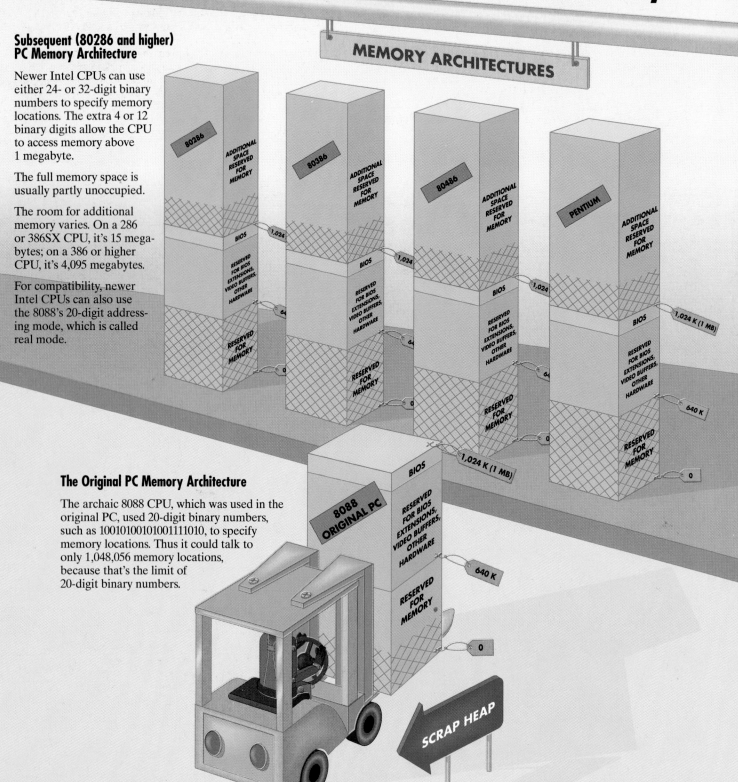

The Original PC Memory Architecture

The archaic 8088 CPU, which was used in the original PC, used 20-digit binary numbers, such as 10010100101001111010, to specify memory locations. Thus it could talk to only 1,048,056 memory locations, because that's the limit of 20-digit binary numbers.

DOS Memory Usage

DOS maintains compatibility with the original PC by continuing to use real mode, even on newer PCs. This enables DOS and DOS applications to run on the entire range of PCs.

Windows Memory Usage

Windows, which runs only on 286-based and newer PCs, instructs the CPU to use all of its memory address bits. This operating mode is called protected mode because use of the CPU's full addressing capability also enables memory protection. Protection means that each program can only access its own memory, and is restricted from accessing other programs' memory. Protection makes a system more reliable. Real mode applications can't run when the CPU is in protected mode, because they don't know how to work with the additional address bits.

MEMORY USAGE

DOS

WINDOWS

Special drivers facilitate limited use of memory beyond 1 megabyte. The two most common drivers are VDISK, which simulates a disk drive using memory, and EMS, or expanded memory drivers, which create a pool of memory buffers for programs to access.

In protected mode on the 386 and newer processors, there is a feature called *virtual-86 emulation*, which mimics real mode. Windows uses virtual-86 mode to run DOS sessions and DOS applications on 386 and newer CPUs. On a 286, Windows switches back to real mode to run DOS.

BIOS

RESERVED FOR BIOS EXTENSIONS, VIDEO BUFFERS, OTHER HARDWARE

1,024 K (1 MB)

640 K

DOS APPLICATION (e.g., 1-2-3)

DOS

0

WINDOWS AND WINDOWS APPLICATIONS

BIOS

1,024 K (1 MB)

RESERVED FOR BIOS EXTENSIONS, VIDEO BUFFERS, OTHER HARDWARE

640 K

WINDOWS AND WINDOWS APPLICATIONS

DOS

0

DOS is present when Windows is running, but it is used only for file operations.

Hatching shows installed memory, which varies from machine to machine

How Windows Boots

THE TERM *to boot* comes from the idea of pulling on your boots first thing in the morning to prepare for the day. When Windows boots, it starts life as a relatively normal DOS program, but it then keeps growing and changing until it has become a full operating system that has wrested control of your PC from DOS.

Windows boots in two phases: First the PC boots to DOS, and then once DOS is running, Windows itself boots, thereby taking over your PC. When your PC is turned on, or when you press Ctrl-Alt-Del on the keyboard, the BIOS (basic input/output system) that is built into your PC gets control. The BIOS copies DOS from disk into memory, and then transfers control to DOS so it can start operating.

DOS's first task is to configure itself and load its optional device drivers. It does this by reading and executing the configuration commands that are stored in the CONFIG.SYS file. Then DOS executes the commands in AUTOEXEC.BAT, which is DOS's start-up batch file. The AUTO-EXEC.BAT file usually contains commands that customize your PC—features such as keyboard enhancers, screen savers, and programs that initialize your internal fax. Often the last command in AUTOEXEC.BAT is WIN, to run Windows. If WIN isn't in your AUTOEXEC.BAT file, then you have to type win when you want to run Windows.

The WIN command starts a short program called WIN.COM, which displays the Windows logo and performs some simple checks to make sure your machine is ready to run Windows. Then WIN.COM runs WIN386.EXE—the heart of Windows. WIN386.EXE switches the CPU to protected mode, which enables advanced features such as the ability to access all of the memory in the machine.

Next, Windows starts down a long path, further configuring and initializing itself every step of the way. Most of the configuration is specified in the SYSTEM.INI file, which is stored in the Windows directory. Early in its trek, Windows loads device drivers for accessing the keyboard and mouse. It also loads its basic fonts, plus the fonts it uses for running DOS applications. If all these steps occur without incident, Windows loads the display driver and then starts to really behave like Windows. The display driver loads last to make it easier for the other drivers to simply type an error message on the screen if they encounter a problem. Once the display driver is in control, messages have to go through Windows, which is a lot more work.

In the last phase of initialization, Windows starts a desktop manager, which is usually Windows's own Program Manager. Each desktop manager has its own way of completing the Windows initialization. Program Manager finishes up by running the start-up applications that are specified in the WINDOWS.INI file, and by starting any applications whose icons are stored in the start-up group. Program Manager's last step is to display its own menus and interfaces, so it's ready to help you use the system.

How Windows Boots

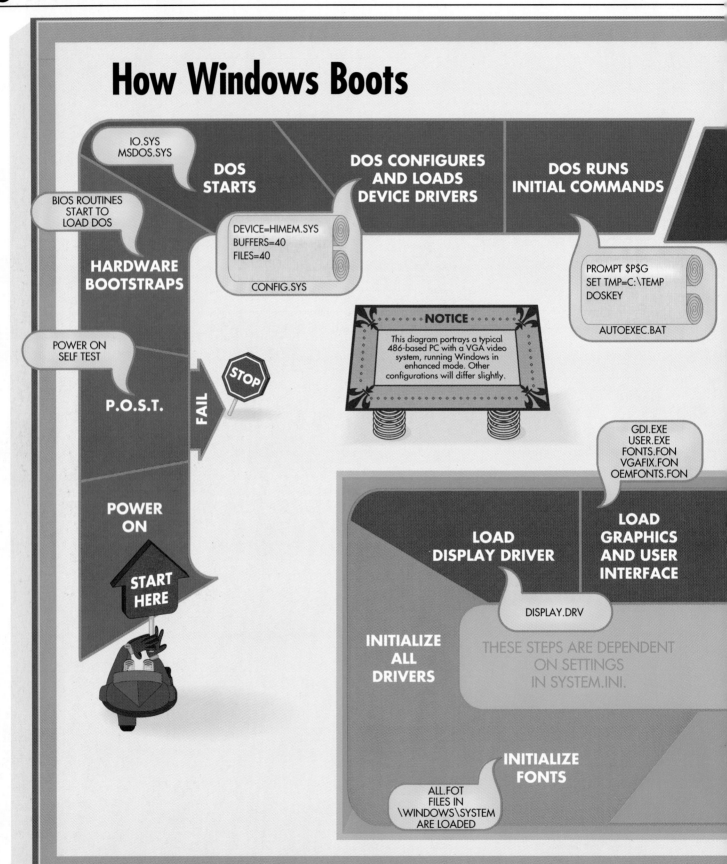

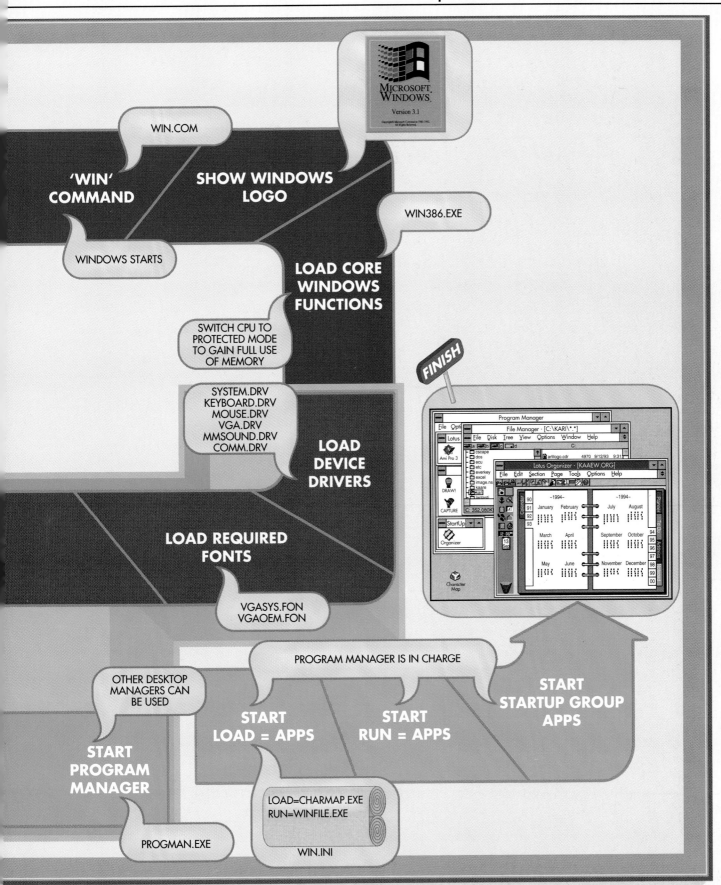

WIN.COM

MICROSOFT WINDOWS
Version 3.1
Copyright© Microsoft Corporation 1985-1992.
All Rights Reserved.

'WIN' COMMAND

SHOW WINDOWS LOGO

WIN386.EXE

WINDOWS STARTS

LOAD CORE WINDOWS FUNCTIONS

SWITCH CPU TO PROTECTED MODE TO GAIN FULL USE OF MEMORY

SYSTEM.DRV
KEYBOARD.DRV
MOUSE.DRV
VGA.DRV
MMSOUND.DRV
COMM.DRV

LOAD DEVICE DRIVERS

FINISH

LOAD REQUIRED FONTS

VGASYS.FON
VGAOEM.FON

PROGRAM MANAGER IS IN CHARGE

OTHER DESKTOP MANAGERS CAN BE USED

START STARTUP GROUP APPS

START LOAD = APPS

START RUN = APPS

START PROGRAM MANAGER

LOAD=CHARMAP.EXE
RUN=WINFILE.EXE

PROGMAN.EXE

WIN.INI

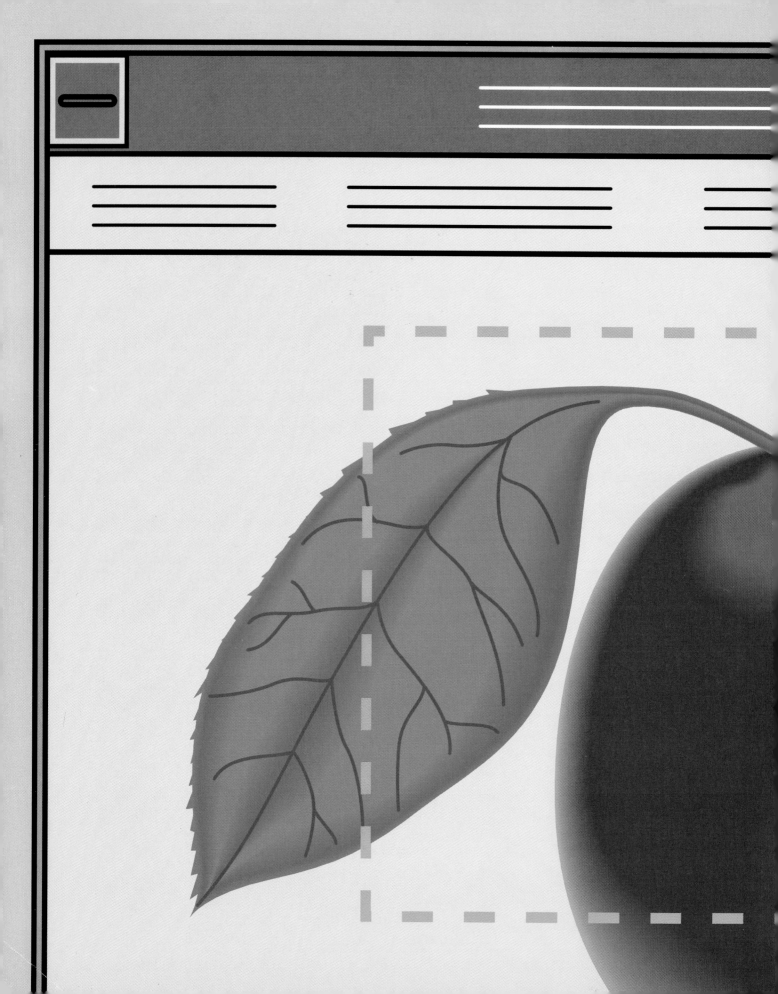

THE GRAPHICAL INTERFACE

CONTENTS

Chapter 4: How the Display Works
24

Chapter 5: How the User Interface Works
32

Chapter 6: How Dialog Boxes Work
42

Chapter 7: How Drawing Works
48

Chapter 8: How Fonts and Typefaces Work
56

Chapter 9: How Cursors and Icons Work
64

APPEARANCES AREN'T EVERYTHING, but in Windows they are important. Windows shields you from the intricacies of the operating environment by providing you with a tidy screen full of objects, whose purpose is intuitive. Instead of making you memorize millions of esoteric commands that you'd have to type, Windows presents you with a manageable set of graphical elements: icons, toolbars, menus, scroll bars, and dialog boxes. Together, these elements, which appear as needed with every Windows step you take, make up the graphical interface.

When you click on a menu item such as File, your action unfurls a pick list of commands for working with your files. When you choose the Scissor icon from a toolbar, you can confidently expect that you'll be involved in a cutting operation on your data or text. These common user interface (UI) components not only help you to use Windows, but they also help software developers by providing an easy-to-use set of standard components.

Although graphics are a central part of Windows, there are many behind-the-scenes tasks, such as managing memory, that are also important. These tasks will be explained later in the book. In this part, we look at exactly what you see when you use Windows: menus, toolbars, status lines, scroll bars, dialog boxes, cursors, icons, bitmaps, and typefaces.

Windows is an event-driven environment. Each keystroke is an event. Every time the mouse moves, that's an event. Every mouse-button click is an event. Each time an event occurs, information about it is sent to the active window so the event can be managed, and an appropriate response can be generated. The event-driven structure of Windows puts you in charge, because you are free to switch from one task to another according to your needs.

Windows's graphical interface facilitates its event-driven core. The graphical interface shows the relationship of the windows to each other, so that you can see just what will happen in response to your events. For example, the active window's title bar is highlighted so you can see where keyboard or mouse events will go. Similarly, windows that can be resized have small notches near the corners of their frames, a visual clue that you can resize the window.

The first four chapters in this part of the book look at UI components. The common element of all these components is that they are managed jointly by Windows and by applications. The application's job is to specify the needed components; for example, applications must specify what selections are present in menus, or what controls are present in dialog boxes. Windows's share of the task is drawing the UI components and managing the user's interaction. Fortunately, Windows has been trained at the factory to know a lot about these components, so it knows just what to do. For example, Windows knows how to draw menus and how to fill a dialog box with UI controls such as list boxes. Windows knows that when you make selections using UI components, it must send a message to the application so the application knows what choices you have made. It's the application's job to respond to these messages by performing the requested task.

The last two chapters in this part of the book detail two big subjects, drawing geometric objects, such as lines and curves, and drawing text. Drawing is everywhere in Windows, from lines, curves, and cursors, to the most complex drawing in Windows, text. Similarly, typefaces are everywhere in Windows, and it's important to understand the basics. These two chapters show you what happens beneath the surface, to create what you see on the screen.

How the Display Works

THE WINDOWS DISPLAY is an information superhighway, routing information from Windows applications directly to you. The display lets you look at numbers and graphs in spreadsheets, it lets you look at the words in a document, and it lets you see the graphics and charts in a presentation.

A more appropriate name for such an environment couldn't be imagined: What you see on the screen is a collection of windows. A window is a rectangular space on your screen that can be used for input or output. In even a simple Windows screen, there are likely to be more windows than you might think. The background of the screen is, itself, a window—the desktop window. The *desktop window* is the parent of all the other windows, and it's only visible where other windows aren't placed on top of it. Each application is composed of at least one window, although most have several windows. It's not surprising that dialog boxes are windows, but you might be surprised to learn that all the controls in the dialog box are themselves windows.

Each window is managed by software so that it has its own look and its own personality. When a window is first displayed, the Windows system asks the window's software to draw its contents. When an event happens within a window, Windows sends the event to the window's software, so that the software can handle the event in any way it deems appropriate. Having software to manage each window is the key to Windows's operation; creating this window-management software is the main activity of Windows software developers.

The difference between a window that's a button and one that's a spreadsheet is, quite simply, the window's management software. For example, when you click on a button in a dialog box, you're actually clicking inside a separate window whose management software makes it act like a button. When the button window's management software is notified of the mouse click event, it redraws the button to look depressed and then it sends an "I've just been pressed" message to the dialog box window. When you click inside a spreadsheet, well, that's a much more complicated story, but again it's the spreadsheet window's management software that determines what happens. The point is that each window has its own behavior and appearance, which is governed by the management software associated with that window.

Even a simple application such as Windows's Notepad accessory may use several windows. In a more complex application, such as Corel PHOTO-PAINT, there are many windows, with a rich set of relationships. To the PHOTO-PAINT program, each window is a separate entity, which means it can tend to each window individually. PHOTO-PAINT relies on Windows to build the composite view of the application by combining all the individual windows.

It's the job of Windows to keep track of all the windows that are in use. This is a big, big job; it's a major part of how Windows spends its working day. Each window belongs to a window class. All windows in a given window class use the same cursor. When minimized, they are all represented by the same icon, and they are all managed by the same window-management software. Windows remembers where each window is located, what has been drawn in each window, and what part of each window is hidden by other windows that are on top.

Windows also keeps track of each window's parent. The *parent* is usually the window that was active just before a new window was created. The desktop is the parent of the main window in most applications; application windows are the parents of most dialog and message windows; and dialog windows are the parents of most control windows. Parentage is important because it dictates what's on top, where windows can be drawn, and where keyboard and mouse input is routed.

Applications don't draw directly on the screen; instead, they draw on their windows and let the Windows system take care of screen output. Output to a window that's not visible is remembered by Windows and is output to the screen when the window becomes visible. Similarly, when a window is only partly visible, Windows draws only the visible part on the screen. And in a few cases, Windows discards its remembered image of a window. So as a last resort, Windows can always ask an application to redraw a window.

When we consider a single window, we see cooperation between application programs and Windows. It's the application's responsibility to draw in the window's *client area*, which is the area that remains after Windows has drawn the border, the title bar, the menu, and the scroll bars. It's also the application's responsibility to process mouse and keyboard input in the window. Windows's responsibility is to draw in the features of the nonclient area and to respond to events that occur in that part of the window. The application's usual role in the nonclient area is to specify which features should be present, although it's possible for an application to draw in this area.

When we consider the whole display, it's Windows that bears all the responsibility. Windows keeps track of how the windows are related to each other, so it knows which windows are on top at each place on the screen. When an application writes to a window that is visible, Windows places the output on the screen. When you move a window, or when you click on a background window to move it to the front, Windows arranges all the redrawing. Applications don't need to worry about whether their windows are hidden or visible, because Windows takes care of those details.

How the Display Works

The desktop window is always the bottom window; it's displayed wherever there are no other windows on top. The desktop is, directly or indirectly, the parent of all the other windows in the system.

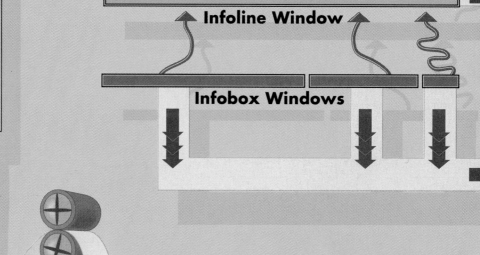

Desktop Window

An Infoline window is used by PHOTO-PAINT to implement its status line, which appears at the bottom of the client window. The Infoline window is mostly hidden by its three children, the Infobox windows. The left and right Infobox windows show status information that is output by PHOTO-PAINT, and the middle shows bar graphs of progress during slow operations like printing. Infoline and Infobox windows are specific to Corel PHOTO-PAINT. Other applications create status lines in other ways, because status lines aren't a standard part of the Windows interface.

Infoline Window

Infobox Windows

The Toolbox window is part of the PHOTO-PAINT application, but for flexibility, its parent is the desktop window, not any of the other PHOTO-PAINT windows. This means the Toolbox can be moved anywhere on the desktop. Perhaps most importantly, the Toolbox isn't subject to commands in the application's Window menu, such as Tile or Cascade, which are intended for managing MDIChild windows.

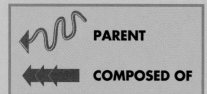

← PARENT

◀◀◀ COMPOSED OF

PHOTO-PAINT is a painting program that's part of the CorelDRAW product. The PHOTO-PAINT main window's nonclient area contains a title bar and menu bar. Its client area, shown shaded in light and dark green, is filled by two windows: an MDIClient window and an Infoline window. The MDIClient window is placed in the top of the client area, shown in light green, and the Infoline window is placed at the bottom of the client area, shown in dark green.

PHOTO-PAINT
Main Window

MDIClient
Window

The MDIClient window is a standard feature of multiple document interface (MDI) applications. An MDI application is one that allows you to have several active windows within the application's own workspace. Most word processors, spreadsheet programs, and drawing packages are MDI applications. The MDIClient window coordinates the child windows, which contain the PHOTO-PAINT documents—the images.

Corel PHOTO-PAINT creates an MDIChild window for each bitmap that you edit. In this figure, the MDIChild window is shown with a title bar and frame drawn by Windows, and with the bitmap image drawn by PHOTO-PAINT.

Windows assembles the PHOTO-PAINT application by placing a title and menu bar on the main window, placing a title bar on the MDIChild and Toolbox windows, and then drawing all the visible parts of the windows on the screen.

[*Continued on next page.*]

How the Display Works

Many applications display information in the client area of their main window. However, the Notepad application is different because it fills its client area with an Edit window—a simple text editor. Edit windows are standard Windows components that any application can use. They are used often, both in simple utilities that contain a text editor, and in dialog boxes where they implement text entry controls. The parent of the Edit window is the Notepad main window.

Program Manager

Desktop Window

Notepad Window

Program Manager Windows

When an application is reduced to an icon, the application icon is drawn in place of its main window. Even though Program Manager is reduced to an icon in this figure, all of its child windows exist and hold their usual contents. They simply aren't drawn on the screen.

The client area of a window is the part of a window that is used by an application. It is what's left over after the border, title bar, menu bar, and scroll bars are drawn. Applications specify which nonclient features they want, but the nonclient features are primarily managed and drawn by Windows itself. In this figure, the client area is shown shaded.

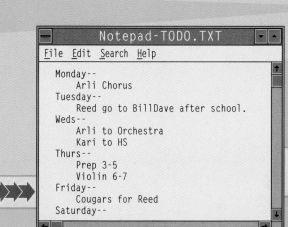

As specified by the Notepad application, Windows assembles the Notepad by drawing a thin frame around the main window, drawing title and menu bars in the main window, drawing horizontal and vertical scroll bars in the main window, and then layering the Edit window on top of the main window's client area.

```
Monday--
    Arli Chorus
Tuesday--
    Reed go to BillDave after school.
Weds--
    Arli to Orchestra
    Kari to HS
Thurs--
    Prep 3-5
    Violin 6-7
Friday--
    Cougars for Reed
Saturday--
```

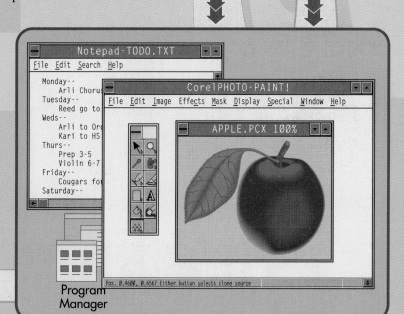

Windows creates the screen display by drawing all the visible parts of all the applications, and by drawing an icon for all the windows that are minimized.

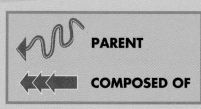

PARENT

COMPOSED OF

How the User Interface Works

THE CONSISTENCY OF Windows's user interface (UI) boosts your productivity. Each time you encounter a new application, you'll find that many features are the same as the applications that you know already. Menus work the same way, and many menu selections, such as File, are nearly universal. Windows are moved and sized the same way, scrolling works the same, and so on.

The UI components built into Windows reflect early- to mid-eighties UI design. At the time Windows was designed, menus, dialog boxes (including list box controls, buttons, check boxes, and text entry controls), scroll bars, and window-sizing controls were the standard components of a modern user interface. These items are still important, but today most applications offer two additional UI components: toolbars and status lines. There isn't any direct support in Windows for toolbars or status lines, although they are relatively easy to create from the raw materials that Windows provides.

Menus are a crucial UI component in most programs, because most programs present their full functionality through their menu. Usually, toolbars and keyboard shortcuts present only a subset of an application's functionality. Programmers build menus by creating a *menu resource*, which is an outlinelike list of menu selections. The menu resource specifies what happens when each menu item is selected. There are two possibilities, either a submenu is displayed or a message is sent to the application that specifies what selection has been made.

Menu resources are stored in the application's executable file in a standardized format. This makes it easy to edit menu resources. Yes, there are mischievous things you can do with the ability to edit menu resources, such as change the menus on a coworker's system. But there's also one serious thing you can do, which is translate a menu into other languages so that an application can serve an international audience.

Toolbars are conceptually similar to menus, but they use pictures instead of text to represent selections. Also, in some applications, toolbars can be positioned anywhere on the screen, so you can place them where they are needed. Applications create a toolbar by first creating a window, and then writing the button images into the window. Applications interact with toolbars in a more primitive manner than they interact with menus. When you click on a button image in a toolbar, the application receives a message that reports the position of the mouse when the button was depressed. It's up to the application to figure out which tool button was pressed, to draw the depressed button, and then to act on the command.

Like toolbars, status bars aren't directly supported by Windows. However, they are a bit easier for an application to manage, because they are used principally for output. Like toolbars, status bars are usually implemented as windows. Applications use status bars by writing text into the status bar window. Chapter 4 showed how Corel PHOTO-PAINT builds its status bars from its Infoline and Infobox windows.

Scroll bars are fully supported by Windows, and there is more to scrolling than you might think. Scroll bars can be drawn anywhere on a window, but usually they are drawn automatically by Windows along the right or bottom edge. The application has to tell Windows what scroll range to use, so that Windows knows how far to move the thumb as you scroll through the document. When you use the scroll bar, Windows sends scroll bar messages to the application. It's up to the application to redraw the display according to what scrolling command was issued.

How Menus Work

5 Windows uses the menu resource to draw the menu in the menu bar.

1 Programmers create a menu by writing a list of all the menu selections in outline format.

NEWSPRINTER

COVER
    4-COLOR
    HEADLINE FONT
PAGE 1
    2-COLOR
    STRIPPED BORDER
PAGE 2
    B/W
    BODY FONT
BACK PAGE
    4-COLOR
    BODY FONT
    STIPPED BORDER

NEWSPRINTER

COVER
    4-COLOR
    HEADLINE FONT
PAGE 1
    2-COLOR
    STRIPPED BORDER

PRINTAPP.EXE

Cover Page 1 Page 2 Back Page

Cover Page 1 Page 2 Back Page

4-Color

Headline Font

2 It's easy to create foreign language translations of menus, because menu resources are stored in a standardized format.

3 The menu is incorporated into the application's .EXE file so that it is easy to access when the program is running.

6 When you click on a menu item, or when you select it with keyboard shortcuts, Windows draws its submenu. Windows remembers what was underneath the menu, so it can be redrawn when the menu is removed.

LOAD NEWSPRINTER

4 When the program is running, it tells Windows what menu to use. Programs can also modify menus while they are running, and they can check or gray menu items.

7 When you make a menu selection that leads to a submenu, Windows draws that submenu. Otherwise, Windows sends a message to the application to tell it what menu item was selected. It is up to the application to respond to the message.

8 When a submenu is removed, Windows restores the area that was hidden.

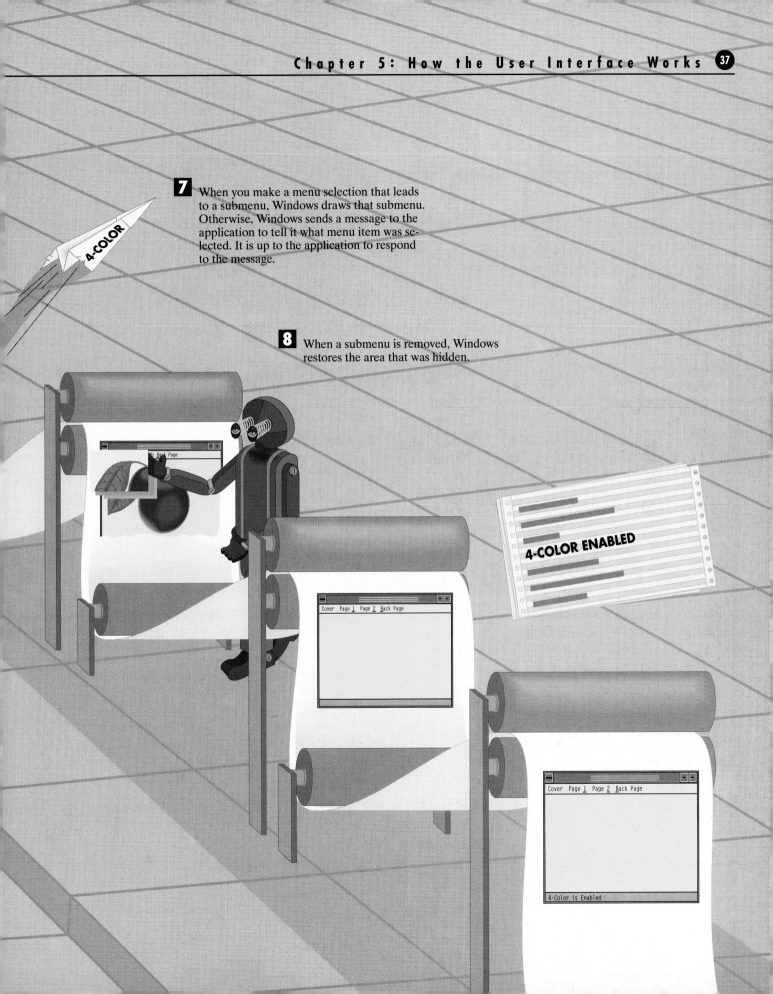

How Toolbars and Status Bars Work

1 The programmer draws the buttons. In some applications, there is one drawing for the whole toolbar, and in other applications there is a separate drawing for each button.

8 When the mouse button is released, Windows sends an LBUTTON_UP message to the application.

9 The application redraws the button to look like it is no longer depressed. If the mouse cursor is still within the bounds of the button, the application must handle the button-press event.

2 The button images are resources that are stored in the application's .EXE file.

LOAD BITMAP (4-COLOR)

3 When the application is running, it can ask Windows to retrieve an image resource, known as a bitmap, from the .EXE file.

5 The application tells Windows to display the toolbar window.

4 The application creates a window for the toolbar, and draws the button images into the window.

LBUTTON_DOWN

6 When the left mouse button is depressed and the mouse cursor is on the toolbar window, Windows sends a LBUTTON_DOWN message to the application.

7 The LBUTTON_DOWN message contains the mouse coordinates. From these coordinates and its record of where it drew the button images in the toolbar, the application determines which button has been clicked. Then the application redraws the button to look depressed.

An application can create a status bar by first creating a window and then asking Windows to display it. An application can output to a status bar at any time.

How Scroll Bars Work

To have horizontal or vertical scroll bars, an application can create a window with either the SB_HSCROLL or SB_VSCROLL style. In this figure, the application has specified the SB_VSCROLL style.

The position of the thumb within the scrollbar indicates what part of the document is visible in the window. You can use the mouse to drag the thumb to scroll to a new position.

You can click the arrow or body to scroll by fixed amounts.

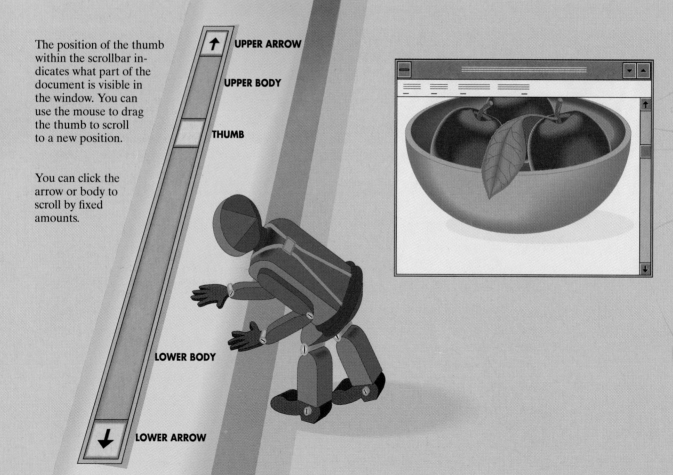

UPPER ARROW

UPPER BODY

THUMB

LOWER BODY

LOWER ARROW

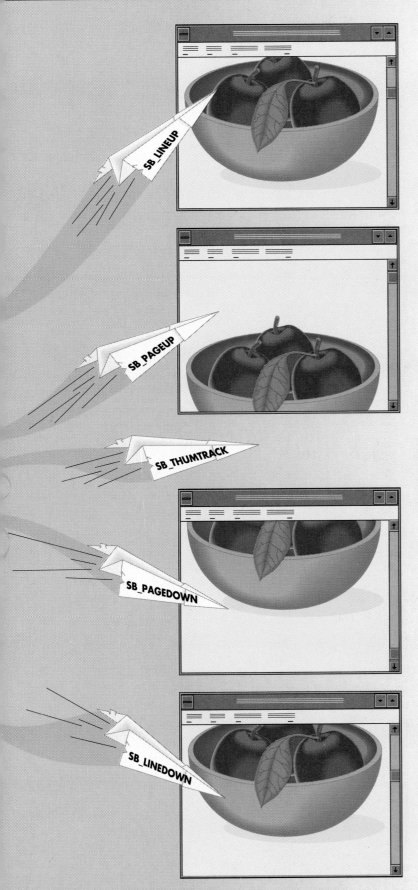

When you click on the upper arrow, Windows sends the SB_LINEUP message to the application. The application responds by scrolling up a small amount.

When you click on the upper body, Windows sends the SB_PAGEUP message to the application. The application responds by scrolling up a page.

When you drag the thumb, Windows sends the application a series of SB_THUMBTRACK messages. The application can respond to these messages, if it wants the window to scroll as you move the thumb. The other option is to ignore SB_THUMBTRACK messages, and then respond to the SB_THUMBPOSITION message, which is sent when the mouse button is released. In this case, the window won't scroll until the thumb is released.

When you click on the lower body, Windows sends the SB_PAGEDOWN message to the application. The application responds by scrolling down a page.

When you click on the lower arrow, Windows sends the SB_LINEDOWN message to the application. The application responds by scrolling down a small amount.

How Dialog Boxes Work

DIALOG BOXES ARE an integral part of the Windows environment. They let you make a set of related choices in a visual, supportive environment. Dialog boxes are constructed from components called controls, which enable you to make choices in your application.

Windows comes equipped with a set of controls that are the basis of most dialog boxes. Some of these standard components are button controls (including push buttons, radio buttons, and check boxes), edit controls, static text controls, list boxes, and scroll bars. But as we saw in Chapter 5, Windows reflects a mid-eighties view of the user interface, and today's cutting edge Windows applications often use additional controls to create a more fluid environment. These custom controls are created by the applications' vendors, and they aren't part of Windows, but they operate much like the built-in controls of Windows.

There are two types of dialog boxes: those that must be closed before you can continue and those that let you switch back to the application's main screen while the dialog box remains visible. The former type, the most common, is called a modal dialog box, because it forces you to switch modes between working in the main part of the application and working in the dialog box. The second type of dialog box, the modeless dialog box, has a less rigid view of modes, because it remains in place even if you switch back to the application, for example the Find dialog box in the Windows Notepad accessory.

Dialog boxes are usually designed with a visual layout tool called a dialog box editor. The editor makes it easy to place and group the controls to create a pleasing appearance. The description of the dialog box's visual characteristics (title, border, size, and so on) together with the list of its controls and their positions is called a dialog resource, and it is placed into the application's .EXE file, just as menu and bitmap resources are stored in the .EXE file.

The most difficult part of dialog box construction from a programmer's perspective is creating the dialog box's management software. Windows provides some of the basic behavior; for example, when you use the Tab key to move from control to control, that's really Windows at work. But in all but the simplest dialog boxes, the programmer must do a lot of work to create a supportive environment for the software user. This work includes initializing the controls so they are ready for work when they first appear, managing interactions between controls, and saving control settings.

Most individual elements in Windows programs are windows; the dialog box itself is a window, and each control within the dialog box is one or more windows. This allows each control to have its own behavior, and also allows each control to send and receive messages.

Sending messages is a key element of how dialog boxes work. Sometimes the messaging is very simple. For example, when you press a button, the button redraws itself to appear depressed, and then it sends an "I've been pressed" message to the dialog box window. Or when you pick a selection in a list box, that selection is redrawn highlighted and then an "Item has been selected" message is sent to the dialog box window.

In many dialog boxes, there is a rich set of interactions between the controls, which is mediated by the dialog box's management software. For example, in many dialog boxes, making a selection by using one control can change other controls. The first control sends notification messages to the dialog box window to tell it what selections you're making, and then the dialog box window's software sends messages to the other controls so they change accordingly.

Designing a Dialog Box

1 Windows contains a set of standard control components.

OK

I

EDIT CONTROLS

BUTTON CONTROLS

LIST BOX CONTROLS

STATIC CONTROLS

COMBO BOX CONTROLS

Radio button control

Static text control

I'M OK DIALOG

YES

NO

MAYBE

2 Programmers use visual design tools to lay out the controls in a dialog box.

3 Dialog resources specify the size and appearance of the dialog box window, together with the size, position, and type of controls. Dialog resources are stored in the application's .EXE file.

4 Custom controls are created by the application vendor. They take a lot of work to create, but once created, they are as easy for the programmer to use as ordinary controls.

PRINTAPP.EXE

PROGRAMMER

5 Programmers write software that manages dialog boxes.

Executing a Dialog Box

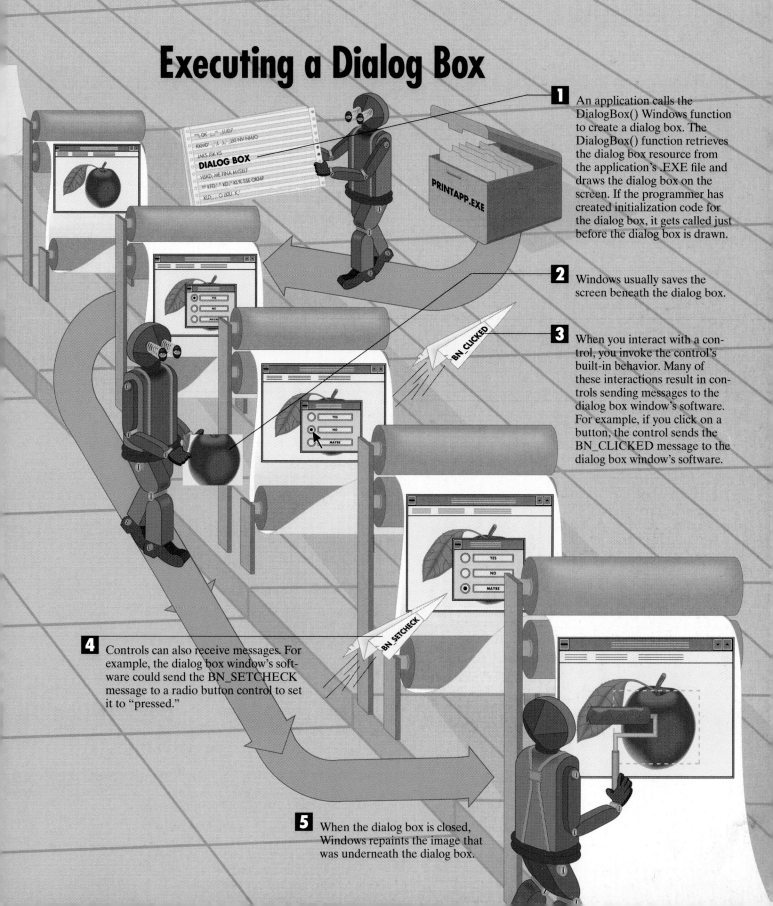

1 An application calls the DialogBox() Windows function to create a dialog box. The DialogBox() function retrieves the dialog box resource from the application's .EXE file and draws the dialog box on the screen. If the programmer has created initialization code for the dialog box, it gets called just before the dialog box is drawn.

2 Windows usually saves the screen beneath the dialog box.

3 When you interact with a control, you invoke the control's built-in behavior. Many of these interactions result in controls sending messages to the dialog box window's software. For example, if you click on a button, the control sends the BN_CLICKED message to the dialog box window's software.

4 Controls can also receive messages. For example, the dialog box window's software could send the BN_SETCHECK message to a radio button control to set it to "pressed."

5 When the dialog box is closed, Windows repaints the image that was underneath the dialog box.

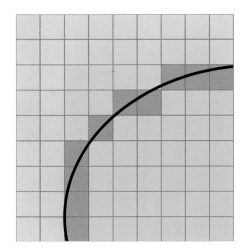

How Drawing Works

WINDOWS EMBODIES a layered approach to drawing. At the lowest level are very basic operations for drawing simple objects such as points, lines, characters, and bitmaps. These low-level functions are the only graphics supplied by Windows, which is surprising considering that Windows is a graphical environment. Layered above the basic drawing operations are more sophisticated graphics operations supplied by applications programs. These more advanced graphical features include Bézier curves, radial and gradient fill patterns, and compatibility with graphics formats such as the TIFF file format. We'll stick to the basics in this chapter, because that's all Windows itself provides. Two closely related topics are discussed in their own chapters: Fonts are discussed in Chapter 8, and cursors and icons are discussed in Chapter 9.

Part of Windows's drawing toolkit is its set of functions for drawing basic geometric shapes, such as rectangles, ellipses, polygons, and arcs. In Windows, these elements are drawn using a *software pen* (see the following illustration). Pens have an adjustable width, color, and style (such as dotted or dashed). If you select a pen color that's not available in the output device, Windows will use the closest available color.

When Windows draws a series of lines, a pen is clearly the tool to use. But what do you do when you draw a rectangle and you want to fill its interior? Or what do you do when you need to draw the background of a whole window? The answer in Windows is a *brush*, which is a software rendering of a paintbrush. Windows brushes come in three styles: solid, hatched, and 8-by-8-patterned brushes, all of which are shown in the accompanying illustration. If an application specifies a solid color that's unavailable in the output device, Windows will simulate that color by using closely spaced points of available colors; this process is called dithering. If an application specifies an unavailable color for a hatched or patterned brush, then Windows will use the closest available color.

When a pen or brush is drawn on a bitmap, Windows can simply copy the pen or brush image exactly onto the surface. But copying is only one possibility. Another option would be to invert the destination wherever the source is colored. If you work out all the possibilities, you'll find there are 16 drawing modes, which are shown in the accompanying illustration.

The second part of Windows's drawing toolkit is its set of functions for working with two-dimensional images; these are called bitmaps. The word *bitmap* reminds us that images are stored in memory cells called bits, and *map* refers to the two-dimensional interpretation of memory used to store images. Each point in a bitmap is called a *pixel*, an abbreviation for picture element.

Another term for *bitmap graphics* is *raster graphics*. The term *raster* comes from the television industry, where it refers to a closely spaced sequence of lines drawn on the TV screen by the electron beam.

Windows contains a flexible set of operations on bitmaps. Some of these operations are the line and other geometric drawing operations that draw into a bitmap. In addition, there are pure bitmap operations that allow bitmaps to be copied, combined, and re-shaped. These operations are called blits, or bitblits, which stands for *bit block transfer*.

Applications programs combine the basic drawing operations to create their own tools and graphics operations. For example, CorelDRAW includes a calligraphic pen that lets you draw on the screen as if you were inking parchment with a real calligraphic pen. Corel's software calligraphic pen is implemented using a complex sequence of low-level raster and vector operations. And, Windows's Paintbrush offers a selection of paintbrushes for you to use. These paintbrushes aren't Windows brushes, but rather they are implemented by Paintbrush using Windows drawing functions to create the illusion of an artist's brush.

How Pens and Brushes Work

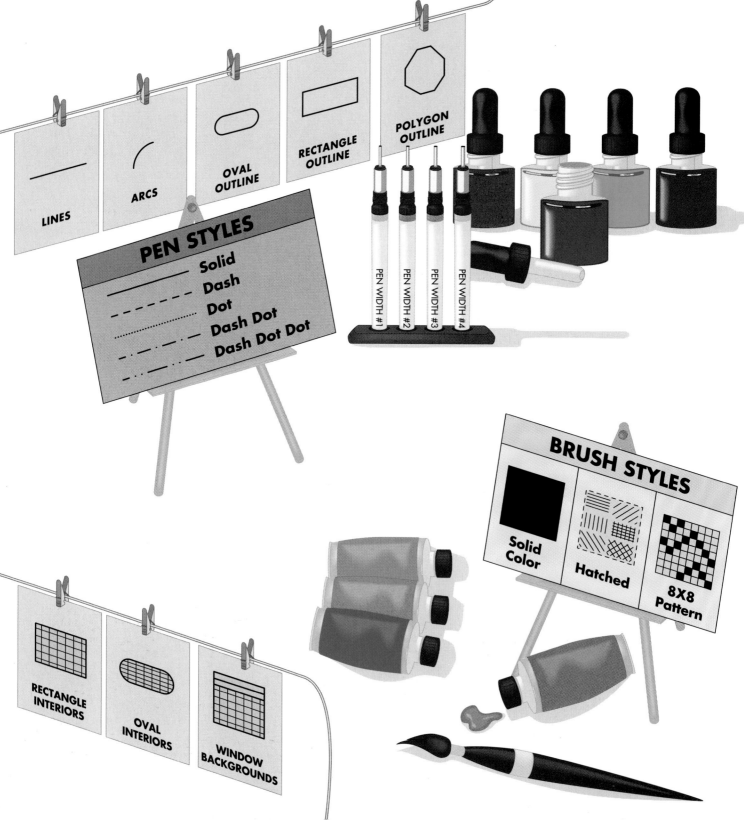

LINES

ARCS

OVAL OUTLINE

RECTANGLE OUTLINE

POLYGON OUTLINE

PEN STYLES

Solid
Dash
Dot
Dash Dot
Dash Dot Dot

PEN WIDTH #1
PEN WIDTH #2
PEN WIDTH #3
PEN WIDTH #4

BRUSH STYLES

Solid Color

Hatched

8X8 Pattern

RECTANGLE INTERIORS

OVAL INTERIORS

WINDOW BACKGROUNDS

Windows Drawing Modes

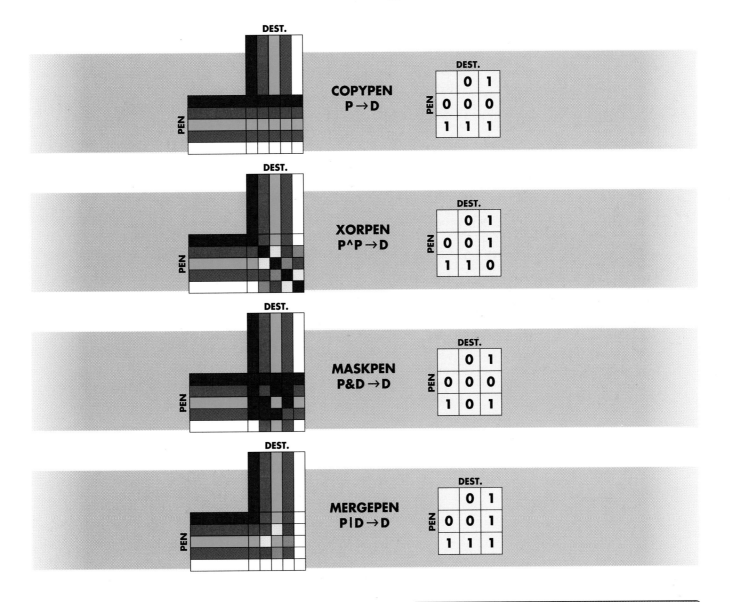

When you draw using a pen on paper, the new ink from your pen completely hides what's below. Although Windows offers this possibility (the COPYPEN drawing mode), it also offers 15 other drawing modes. These additional Windows drawing modes resemble painting with watercolors; the new color combines in some way with the color underneath. (The 16 drawing modes are the four modes shown above, plus the 12 in the table to the right.)

OTHER WINDOWS DRAWING MODES

BLACK	Ø→D		MASKPENNOT	P&~D→D
WHITE	1→D		MASKNOTPEN	~P&D→D
NOT	~D→D		NOTMASKPEN	~(P&D)→D
NOP	D→D		MERGENOTPEN	~P│D→D
NOTCOPYPEN	~P→D		MERGEPENNOT	P│~D→D
NOTXORPEN	~(P^D)→D		NOTMERGEPEN	~(P│D)→D

How Lines, Circles, Ellipses, and Arcs Are Drawn

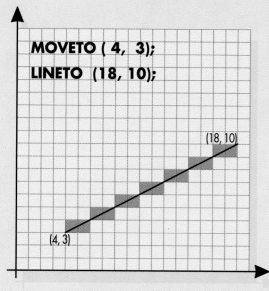

MOVETO (4, 3);
LINETO (18, 10);

(18, 10)

(4, 3)

How Lines Are Drawn

Lines are drawn in a bitmap with a Windows pen. In this example, the pen has drawn a line from the point (4, 3) to the point (18, 10). Each square in the grid is a single pixel, which is the smallest area that can be colored. The theoretical line is shown in black, but this line can't be drawn exactly because only whole pixels can be drawn. Therefore, Windows draws its best approximation of the perfect line, which is shown in dark orange.

The stair-step appearance is called aliasing. Many applications avoid the appearance of aliasing by using shades of gray to trick the eye into seeing a smoother edge.

How Circles and Ellipses Are Drawn

Windows outlines circles and ellipses using a pen, and optionally, Windows fills their interiors using a brush. Circles and ellipses are specified by their bounding rectangle, which is shown in light orange in this figure. The perfect ellipse is shown in black, but it can't be drawn exactly, so its best approximation is shown in dark orange

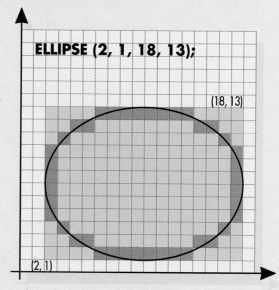

ELLIPSE (2, 1, 18, 13);

(18, 13)

(2, 1)

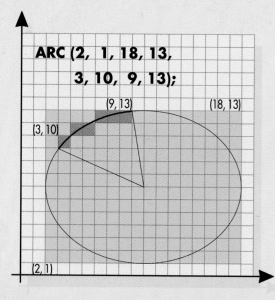

ARC (2, 1, 18, 13,
3, 10, 9, 13);

(9, 13)   (18, 13)

(3, 10)

(2, 1)

How Arcs Are Drawn

Arcs are sections of ellipses, which are drawn using a Windows pen. They are specified by their bounding rectangle, which is shown in light orange, and by the starting and ending coordinates of the displayed segment.

How Bitmaps Are Drawn

Source Bitmap

A *bitmap* is a region of memory that is interpreted as an image. This 19-by-12 bitmap might have been read from a file, or created on the fly using simple drawing commands.

BITBLT Copy

The simplest bit block transfer (BITBLT) is a copy.

Stretch BITBLT

BITBLT Src & Dst →Dst

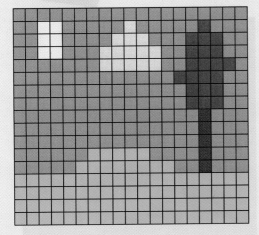

Stretch BITBLTs can change the dimension of a bitmap. When you stretch a bitmap, Windows combines or duplicates pixels as necessary to form the new image.

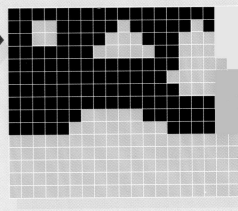

BITBLTs can use any of 256 drawing modes. This picture shows an AND operation between source and destination bitmaps. If the destination is originally pure green, then the AND operation will produce green output only where the source contains green. In this figure, the yellow sun, the green grass, the green leaves, and the white cloud all contain green; other colors become black.

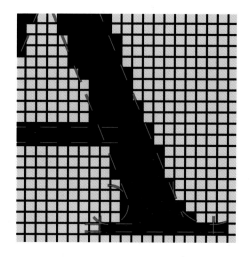

How Fonts and Typefaces Work

TYPOGRAPHY IS A 500-year-old art that has rapidly become an integral part of the Windows environment. Just a few years ago, computers could print text, but usually in only one size and style. But today, both computer hardware and software—like typographers—have a richer view of text.

A typeface is a style of type, such as Times Roman or Courier. An assortment of letters, numbers, punctuation marks, and so on, of a particular typeface, in a specific size, and with a certain attribute is called a font. For example, 10-point Times Roman italic and 14-point Courier bold are fonts. Note, however, that in Windows and most Windows applications, the term *font* is often used mistakenly for *typeface*. For example, many Windows programs use a Font list box to select a typeface. This misnomer has taken root in the Windows world.

Fonts are always a specific size, which is usually specified in points. A point is very nearly a 72nd of an inch. (It's not exactly a 72nd, but it's so close that you can think of it as a 72nd of an inch.) Thus 72-point type is 1 inch tall; 12 points is a common type size that is about ⅙ inch. The individual lines that make up a type character are called *strokes*. For example, a *T* is composed of two strokes. The small lines at the end of the strokes are *serifs*; typefaces without serifs are called *sans serif* typefaces.

A *character set* is a group of symbols, with a specific position for each character in the group. For example, the capital *A* is in position 65 in all the Windows text character sets. In Windows 3.1 there are two character sets for text, plus the Symbol character set for mathematical and other special-purpose symbols. Windows uses two text character sets: ANSI and OEM. The ANSI (American National Standards Institute) character set is the primary character set of Windows. Its first half follows the older ASCII (American Standard Code for Information Interchange) set, and its second half contains 128 additional symbols, including most accented European characters. The Windows ANSI character set is nearly identical to the International Standards Organization's (ISO's) Latin1 character set.

The OEM (original equipment manufacturer) character set is a Windows version of the character set built into the IBM PC and its clones. (The term *OEM* was invented by Microsoft as a substitute for the term *IBM*, which is a registered trademark of the International Business

Machines Corporation.) As in all PC video adapters, the first 128 characters of the OEM set follow the ASCII plan, and the next 128 include some accented European characters, Greek letters, and line-drawing characters that are used to draw borders in many MS-DOS applications. Windows uses the OEM character set primarily for communication programs and for DOS windows.

The ANSI and OEM character sets each have 256 positions. This is enough to store the letters, digits, and punctuation marks used in the United States, and perhaps barely enough to store the letters (plain and accented), digits, and punctuation marks used in Europe. But it is far too small a limit for many languages, such as Chinese. The solution to this problem is Unicode, which is a single character set that encompasses all the symbols used by all the languages of the world, modern as well as ancient. Unicode can handle 65,536 separate characters. This means that every character in each language has its own position. Unicode isn't supported by Windows 3.1, but it is the primary character set of Windows NT, and should be supported in future versions of Windows.

Windows uses three different typeface formats: raster, vector, and outline. Raster typeface technology is the simplest and fastest. For each raster font, the bitmap images of all the characters are stored in a file. When the font is used, the bitmaps for each character are retrieved and then drawn (BITBLT'd) on the screen. Raster fonts operate efficiently because Windows doesn't have much to do, and they look great because they are hand drawn. Windows uses raster fonts for tasks where speed is essential, such as the text of menus and dialog boxes, and for the screen fonts in DOS windows. Raster fonts are usually avoided in documents and drawings where high-quality output to any printer or screen is required.

Windows can scale raster fonts, but only by repeating rows or columns of the bitmap image. This process quickly produces *jaggies* (rough-edged curves and stair-stepped diagonal lines). To avoid the jaggies, raster fonts are supplied in multiple sizes, often 10, 12, 14, 18, and 24 points. You also need different versions of raster fonts for each different output device resolution. For example, a 12-point raster font for a 72-dot-per-inch (dpi) output device, such as many VGA display screens, would be 6 (72 divided by 12) pixels tall. The same twelve point font for a 300-dpi printer would need to be 25 pixels tall. Because raster fonts are designed for specific output device resolutions, their names usually include a three-letter device name as part of the font name. For example, VGASYS.FON is the name of a VGA resolution version of the Windows system font.

Vector typefaces, also known as stroke typefaces, are composed of line segments; they are intended for use on plotters and other output devices that do not support bitmap operations. The three stroke typefaces supplied with Windows are Roman, Modern, and Script. You can use these typefaces on the screen, but you probably shouldn't (because they look thin and limp) unless you are readying a drawing for output to a plotter.

Outline typefaces are the newest typeface technology in Windows. In an outline typeface, the shape of each symbol is represented mathematically as a series of lines and curves. When a symbol is needed, the outline typeface software has to consult the outline file to get the description of the shape. Then the software must *rasterize* (draw) the symbol in a bitmap, scaled to the desired size, according to the output device's resolution. The same typeface description can serve for both displays and printers, because device resolution is accounted for during rasterization. Once a symbol is in a bitmap, it can be rapidly copied to screen or printer as if it were a symbol from a simple raster font. Also, the rasterizing software temporarily retains the bitmaps of often-used symbols so that in subsequent use an outline symbol operates about as efficiently as a symbol from a raster font.

At small point sizes, outline fonts are sometimes less legible than raster fonts. That's because designers of raster fonts can handcraft every pixel of every symbol for best legibility. When an outline typeface is rendered in a small point size, there are very few pixels to represent the shape. Slavishly following the formulas may produce the mathematically best fit in the available pixels, but it may not be the best for viewing. That's why outline typefaces usually contain *hints*, which suggest how to draw the symbols in small sizes. For example, a hint might suggest that both vertical segments of an *H* should be the same width. The hint would be irrelevant for an *H* whose strokes averaged 50 pixels wide, because you wouldn't notice the difference between a 51-pixel-wide stroke and a 50-pixel-wide stroke. But a hint that both verticals of the *H* should be the same size would be crucial for an *H* whose strokes were just a few pixels wide, because you would easily see the difference between a stroke that is 1 pixel wide and one that is 2 pixels wide.

The first outline typeface support for Windows came from companies that specialize in typesetting software, including Adobe, Bitstream, and Agfa. The most successful of these early efforts was Adobe and its Type 1 typeface standard. Over 20,000 Type 1 typefaces exist, which makes it a rich resource for professional typographers.

Microsoft introduced TrueType outline typeface support in Windows 3.1. TrueType was developed jointly by Apple and Microsoft to provide a common typeface system for the Macintosh and Windows environments. TrueType has capabilities similar to those of earlier outline typeface systems such as Adobe's Type 1 standard, but it has the advantage of being an integral part of the two major desktop software platforms.

Type Sizes and Character Sets

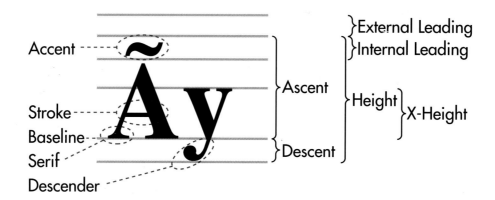

The OEM character set is the same as the traditional character set in PC video adapters. It contains the ASCII characters in the first half (the first three rows shown in the Character Map utility) and it contains line-drawing, Greek, and some accented characters of languages spoken in Europe in the second half.

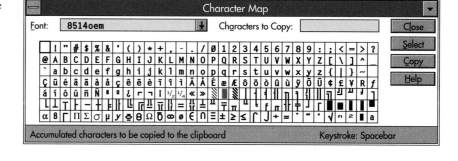

The ANSI character set, which is nearly identical to the ISO Latin1 character set, provides symbols and accented characters of languages spoken in Europe in its second half. Note that the position of accented characters in the ANSI character set is different from that of the OEM character set. A document prepared using one character set but displayed using another will appear as gibberish if characters from the second half of the character set are used.

Raster Typefaces

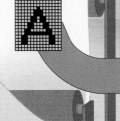

vgasys.fon

Symbol images are read from files and stored in bitmaps in system memory.

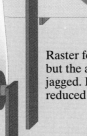

Symbols are drawn using BITBLT operations.

Raster fonts can be enlarged, but the appearance becomes jagged. Raster fonts can't be reduced in size.

Raster fonts are used for menus, DOS sessions, and other performance-sensitive tasks. Their poor scalability makes them a bad choice for text that will be printed, unless you have printer versions of all the raster fonts that you use.

Stroke Typefaces

Stroke typefaces are drawn into a bitmap using Windows line-drawing commands.

roman.fon

Stroke typefaces are stored in files that contain lists of line segments that specify how to draw each symbol.

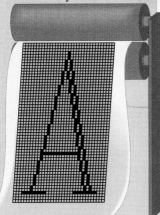

Stroke typefaces can be scaled, but they remain thin because they don't contain any width or fill information. Regardless of what size a Roman letter A is drawn, it consists of six thin line segments.

Windows 3.1 contains three stroke typefaces: Roman, Script, and Modern. These typefaces should only be used if your output device is a plotter.

Outline Typefaces

TrueType outline typefaces use an .FOT file to store basic information about a typeface. The .FOT file also stores the name of the file that contains the typeface's outline data. (For Type 1 typefaces, the analogous file is .PFM.)

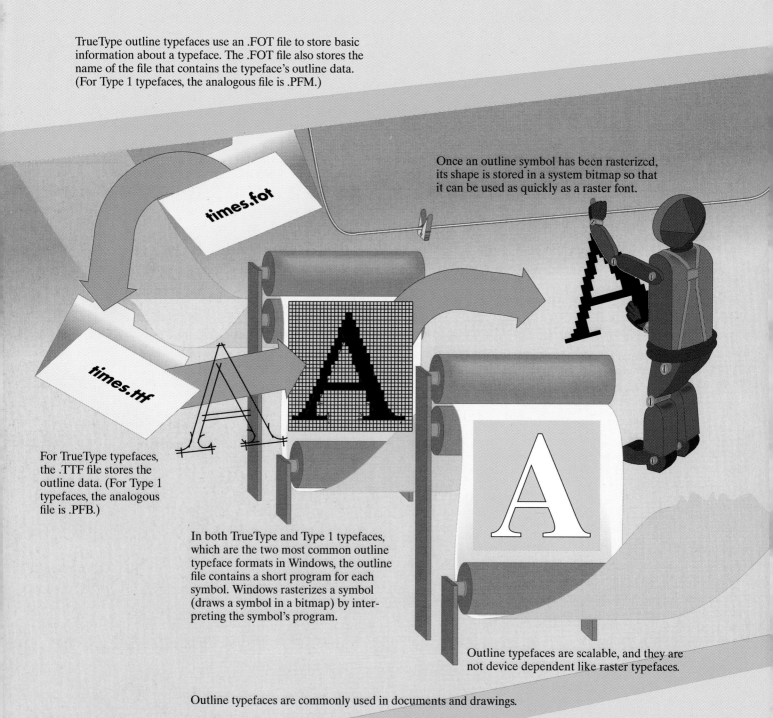

Once an outline symbol has been rasterized, its shape is stored in a system bitmap so that it can be used as quickly as a raster font.

For TrueType typefaces, the .TTF file stores the outline data. (For Type 1 typefaces, the analogous file is .PFB.)

In both TrueType and Type 1 typefaces, which are the two most common outline typeface formats in Windows, the outline file contains a short program for each symbol. Windows rasterizes a symbol (draws a symbol in a bitmap) by interpreting the symbol's program.

Outline typefaces are scalable, and they are not device dependent like raster typefaces.

Outline typefaces are commonly used in documents and drawings.

Outline Typeface Hinting

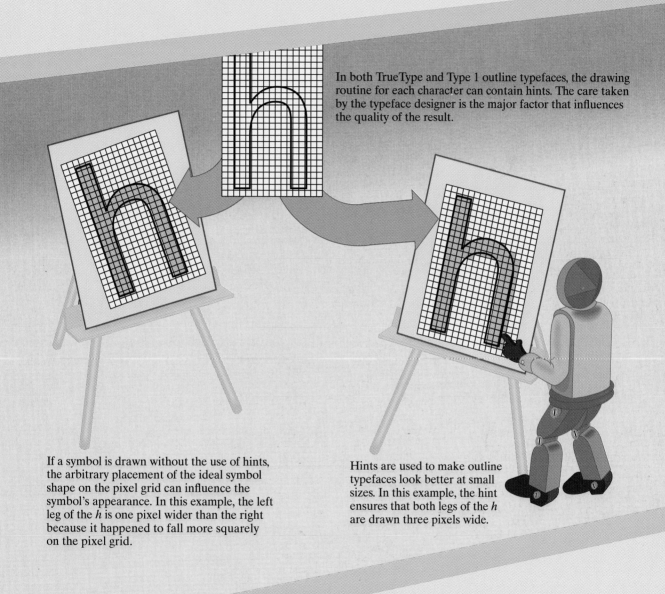

In both TrueType and Type 1 outline typefaces, the drawing routine for each character can contain hints. The care taken by the typeface designer is the major factor that influences the quality of the result.

If a symbol is drawn without the use of hints, the arbitrary placement of the ideal symbol shape on the pixel grid can influence the symbol's appearance. In this example, the left leg of the *h* is one pixel wider than the right because it happened to fall more squarely on the pixel grid.

Hints are used to make outline typefaces look better at small sizes. In this example, the hint ensures that both legs of the *h* are drawn three pixels wide.

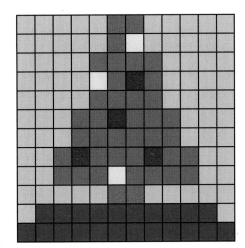

CHAPTER

9

How Cursors and Icons Work

CONS HELP MAKE Windows easy to use. They enable you to start a program simply by pointing and clicking. Icons also simplify your work while you're using an application program. For example, if you're working with several spreadsheets using Quattro Pro for Windows, you can switch from one sheet to another by clicking on an icon. In a way, icons make your Windows desktop into an old-fashioned rolltop desk with lots of small drawers and compartments. Clicking on an icon is like opening one of the small drawers and placing its contents on the desktop. Reducing a program or document to an icon is like putting something away in one of your desk's small compartments.

Cursors are less touted than icons, but they too are an important part of the Windows interface. The fact that you might not have noticed all the times your cursor changed shape only indicates how well it's doing its job. The role of the cursor isn't to call attention to itself, but rather to help you focus on the task at hand.

Cursors and icons are discussed together because they work—deep inside Windows at least—very similarly. Both cursors and icons are stored as pairs of bitmaps, and both can be moved by the mouse across the screen. Also, Windows keeps track of which cursor and which icon to use for each window. One more similarity is that both icons and cursors are Windows resources. A few standard cursor and icon resources are stored in Windows itself; an application's own cursors and icons are stored in the application's .EXE file.

Icon and cursor resources both consist of two bitmaps. For both icons and cursors, the first is a monochrome bitmap that stores the shape of the icon or cursor. This bitmap is called the AND bitmap because it is BITBLIT'd onto the display using a logical AND operation, as shown in the illustration. For a cursor, the second bitmap is a monochrome bitmap, and for an icon, the second bitmap contains the color image. For both icons and cursors, the second bitmap is called an XOR bitmap because it is BITBLIT'd onto the screen using an exclusive OR operation.

The major difference between cursors and icons—besides that icons are brightly colored and cursors are not—is how they are used. A cursor is what you see on the screen as you move the pointer. As the cursor moves from one window to another, Windows automatically updates its shape according to which cursor has been registered for each window. Applications can also change the cursor; for example, they can switch to the hourglass cursor during a long operation. There are two types of icons, document icons and application icons. *Application icons* are drawn on the desktop, and they represent active applications, except for Program Manager, which draws application icons in its group windows so that you can click on them to start applications. *Document icons* are drawn inside an application's main window, and they usually represent documents (such as a spreadsheet or drawing). When you reduce an application or a document to an icon, Windows draws an icon in place of the document or application. This saves space on the screen so you have more room to work on something else. When you want to resume work with the reduced application or document, you can double-click on its icon and Windows will switch back to its previous display.

Like cursors, icons can be dragged across the screen, but that's just to allow you to position them wherever you want. Your major interaction with icons is pointing at them and then clicking, either once or twice. One click will bring forth a menu with choices such as Restore, Maximize, and Close. Double-clicking on an icon either starts or resumes an application, or it restores a document that was temporarily reduced to an icon.

Windows comes equipped with a variety of standard cursors and icons. Its standard cursors include the ubiquitous arrow pointer, the I-beam cursor used for most text editing, and the four double-ended arrows that are used for sizing windows. And the hourglass cursor tells us it's time to wait. The Windows kernel contains only a few standard icons, such as the question mark icon that is used in some message boxes. However, you'll find a rich collection of standard icons in Windows's Program Manager application. Most people use Program Manager's icons to represent DOS applications, because DOS applications usually don't provide their own Windows icon. You can also use Program Manager's icons to represent Windows applications, but this is seldom necessary because Windows applications have their own icons.

How Cursors Work

1 Cursors are stored in two bitmaps. The AND bitmap contains the cursor shape.

The hot spot

The AND bitmap

The XOR bitmap

2 The XOR cursor bitmap shows how the cursor is filled in.

3 The AND bitmap is BITBLIT'd to the screen using the AND logical operation. Zeroes in the AND bitmap erase the image underneath the cursor.

4 The XOR bitmap is BITBLIT'd to the screen using the Exclusive OR logical operation. Pixel values of one inside the XOR bitmap usually specify white, and zeroes usually specify black. (Outside the cursor shape, one specifies inversion and zero specifies transparency.)

5 When you move the pointer, Windows redraws the cursor in the new location, and sends a WM_MOUSEMOVE message to the window below the cursor. The message indicates the on-screen location of the cursor's hot spot. If a mouse button is clicked or double-clicked, the appropriate message is sent to the window.

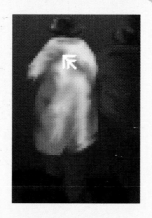

How Icons Work

The AND bitmap

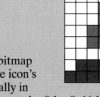

The XOR bitmap

1 Icons are stored in two bitmaps. The AND bitmap contains the icon's shape.

2 The XOR bitmap contains the icon's image, usually in color. Icons may be 8-by-8, 16-by-16, or 32-by-32 pixels.

3 First, the icon's AND bitmap is BITBLIT'd to the screen using the AND logical operation. Zeroes in the AND bitmap erase the image underneath the icon.

4 Next, the icon's XOR bitmap is BITBLIT'd to the screen using the Exclusive OR logical operation.

5 When you reduce an application or a document to an icon, Windows replaces the application or document window with its associated icon.

TREES.PCX

6 When you double-click on an icon, Windows switches back to the window that's represented by the icon.

THE BUILT-IN WINDOWS UTILITIES

CONTENTS

Chapter 10: How Program Manager Works
74

Chapter 11: How File Manager Works
80

Chapter 12: How the Control Panel Works
86

Chapter 13: How Windows Help Works
92

WINDOWS IS CALLED an environment because it provides a setting in which applications programs can operate. Most of this book focuses on the environment part of Windows, which provides application programs with graphics routines, printer drivers, menu functions, dialog-box functions, and so on. In this role, Windows is much like a grand playhouse; it provides a stage for the players and seats for the audience.

But Windows is also like the actors on the playhouse stage: Windows provides a collection of utility programs. Some of these utility programs, such as Program Manager and File Manager, play a key part in most people's Windows day. Others, such as Control Panel and Print Manager, are important for managing the Windows environment.

The difference between a utility and an application is that an application program focuses on the end result. For example, the role of the CorelDRAW application is to help you make a drawing, and the role of the Quattro Pro application is to help you construct a spreadsheet. Program Manager and File Manager are utilities, and like other utilities, they focus more on managing the computer system itself; they help you use your computer and they are vital to your work, but they don't directly produce the end result.

In addition to its collection of utilities, Windows also provides a trio of miniapplications, Windows Write, Windows Terminal, and Windows Paintbrush. These small application programs provide rudimentary word processing, telecommunications, and painting. Most users who are heavily involved in one of these three tasks buy a full-featured commercial package for that purpose, but the supplied programs are useful for occasional work and are appreciated by those on a tight budget.

In this part of the book we're going to examine four of the utilities that are supplied with Windows: Program Manager, File Manager, Control Panel, and Windows Help. Program Manager and File Manager deserve attention because they access your applications and files. Program Manager lets you start applications by clicking on icons; File Manager provides a visual environment for working with files; and Control Panel lets you customize the Windows environment. For example, Control Panel allows you to specify desktop colors, time and date formats, and mouse sensitivity. Control Panel is explained because understanding how it works will help you understand how Windows works. Windows Help is covered because it is used by most Windows programs to provide a help facility.

What's common to all the Windows utilities is that they are standard Windows programs. Though these programs perform tasks that seem specialized, like managing files, starting programs, or viewing help documents they follow standard Windows rules and exhibit standard Windows behavior.

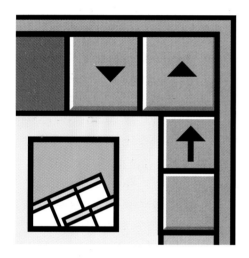

How Program Manager Works

PROGRAM MANAGER, which displays an icon for each program, is a visual, point-and-click utility for starting programs or applications. If you double-click on an application's icon, the application starts to execute so you can use the program. Program Manager helps make Windows easy to use, because it lets you run programs without typing commands.

Program Manager is partly an ordinary Windows program and partly a special utility that performs a unique role. Let's look first at the unique role. When Windows first boots, it assembles itself from all its components, as shown in Chapter 2. Once all the supporting players are ready, Windows enters the last phase of its boot process, which is starting a user interface shell. In most Windows installations, the user interface shell is Program Manager, although some people prefer one of the snazzier replacements, such as Norton Desktop for Windows. So one unique trait of Program Manager is that it usually starts automatically, as the last phase of the Windows boot process. And, when you exit from Program Manager, you automatically end your Windows session. Thus, you should only close Program Manager after you've saved all your work in your application and you're finished using Windows.

In between booting and shutting down, Program Manager behaves like an ordinary Windows program. Of course, its role, starting other Windows programs, is unusual. But Program Manager behaves like an ordinary Windows citizen while performing that task.

Program Manager organizes applications into groups. Each group is displayed in a window that contains a set of application icons. You can view a group window, which lets you see the individual icons, or you can reduce a group window to an icon, so there's room to look at other groups. Program Manager stores information about each group in a .GRP file in the Windows directory.

When you install Windows you'll automatically get a Main group for some of the major utilities, an Accessories group for the remaining utilities, a StartUp group that lets you specify applications that automatically start each time you start Windows, and a Games group. Program Manager's File-New menu selection lets you create new groups.

When you install commercial Windows software, each package usually makes its own group. You can use the groups provided by your applications, or you can move application icons into your own groups. For example, you could move all of your business applications into a Business group, all your games into a Games group, and all your children's software into a Kids group.

For each of its program icons, Program Manager keeps track of a few key pieces of information. Most importantly, Windows remembers which application .EXE file should be started when you double-click on an icon. It also remembers which directory to use for each application, and what title should be drawn underneath the icon. You can see and/or specify this information by selecting an icon (click once, not twice) and then choosing the File-Properties menu selection, which brings up the Program Item Properties dialog box. When you make changes using the Program Item Properties dialog box, they will be remembered from one Windows session to another because the information is stored in the .GRP file.

Some people are confused by the difference between an icon that appears inside the Program Manager window, and one that appears on the desktop outside of Program Manager. When an icon is displayed on the desktop, it represents a running program. In the accompanying illustration, the Lotus Organizer icon in the bottom left of the desktop shows that Organizer is active and running, although it has been reduced to an icon to make room for other windows on the screen. In contrast, all the icons visible inside Program Manager represent programs that can be started; these programs are not necessarily active right now, although they might be. If you look closely in the Lotus group and the StartUp group, you'll see icons for Organizer. If you double-click on either icon, you'll start another copy of Organizer, whereas if you double-click on the Organizer icon on the desktop you'll restore the already-running Organizer.

How Program Manager Works

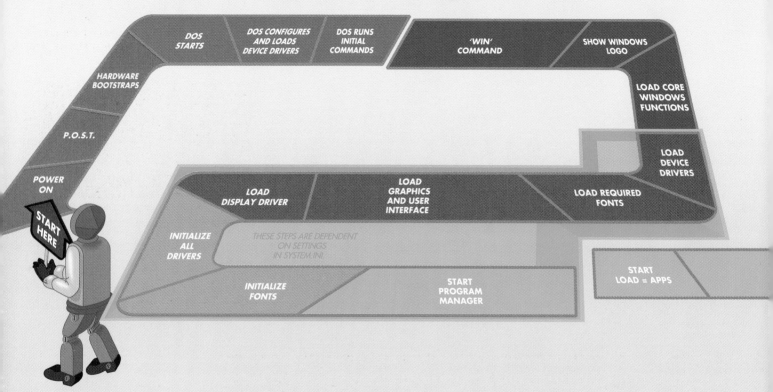

START HERE

DOS STARTS	DOS CONFIGURES AND LOADS DEVICE DRIVERS	DOS RUNS INITIAL COMMANDS		'WIN' COMMAND	SHOW WINDOWS LOGO

HARDWARE BOOTSTRAPS

LOAD CORE WINDOWS FUNCTIONS

P.O.S.T.

LOAD DEVICE DRIVERS

POWER ON

LOAD DISPLAY DRIVER

LOAD GRAPHICS AND USER INTERFACE

LOAD REQUIRED FONTS

INITIALIZE ALL DRIVERS

THESE STEPS ARE DEPENDENT ON SETTINGS IN SYSTEM.INI

INITIALIZE FONTS

START PROGRAM MANAGER

START LOAD = APPS

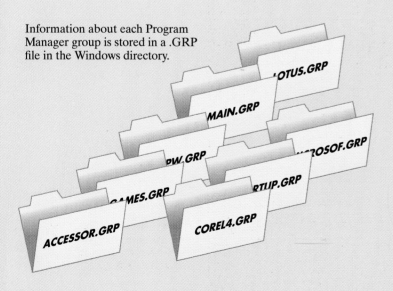

Information about each Program Manager group is stored in a .GRP file in the Windows directory.

LOTUS.GRP

MAIN.GRP

PW.GRP

MICROSOF.GRP

GAMES.GRP

RTUP.GRP

ACCESSOR.GRP

COREL4.GRP

When Program Manager is started, it automatically starts all of the applications in the StartUp group.

Group windows can be reduced to an icon so there's room to view other groups.

Application icons on the desktop represent running programs. They are not managed by Program Manager.

When you double-click on an application icon, Program Manager asks Windows to start that application. Windows loads the application's .EXE file into memory and starts it.

Program Manager is usually started in the last phase of booting. When you exit Program Manager, Windows stops executing.

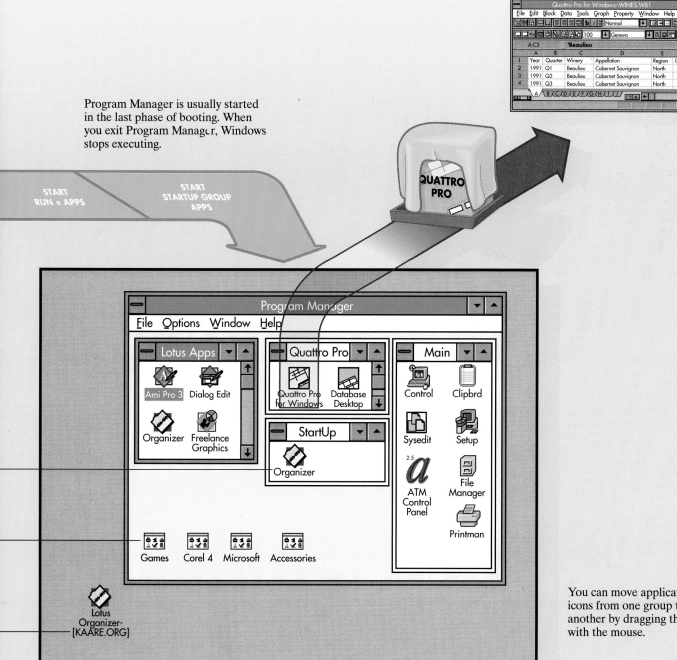

You can move application icons from one group to another by dragging them with the mouse.

How File Manager Works

FILE MANAGER IS a Windows utility that helps you organize your files. File management encompasses several tasks, such as formatting floppy disks and creating directories, but the primary task is searching for files and placing them in appropriate locations.

Files are the major resource of desktop computers. Whatever task you do with your computer, you're working with files. Suppose you use your computer to write a letter. The letter is stored in a file, as is the application you use to write the letter. If you print the letter, you may use several fonts, which are also stored in files. Then there are the dozen or so files that are loaded to form Windows when it first boots, plus the handful of files that compose DOS, plus all the Windows .INI files that store configuration information, and so on. Yes, keeping your files organized is very important.

Fortunately, most file management is done for you automatically. For example, when you install an application the installation software customarily makes all the necessary directories and puts all the application's files in the right places. Unless you're switching to a new computer or installing larger or additional disks, you can usually leave an application in its place. In contrast, your document and data files often need to be moved about as your needs change. If you're sharing a document with a coworker, you might do so by copying it to a floppy disk and giving the floppy disk to the coworker. Or perhaps you might share a document with a coworker by copying it to a shared directory on your network. If your e-mail directory starts to get too crowded, you could make a new e-mail directory for letters received only during the first quarter of the year. File Manager can help you perform these sorts of chores.

File Manager can be started automatically along with Windows if you drag its icon to Program Manager's StartUp group, or you can start it by double-clicking on its icon, which is usually in Program Manager's Main group. When File Manager starts to execute, it consults the WINFILE.INI configuration file. WINFILE.INI stores the names of the directories that File Manager is displaying so that each time File Manager starts, it resumes from just where you left off. (This feature is enabled or disabled using the Save Settings on Exit selection in the Options menu.)

File Manager is a multiwindow application. Each window contains information about one group of files. If you have several windows open, you might want to use the Tile or Cascade selection on the

File menu so you can see all the windows at once. You can use the disk drive icons to switch a window from one drive to another, and you can click on directories to move within a disk's directory system.

If you want to move several files from one directory to another, the easiest way is to open a File Manager window for each directory. Then you can use the mouse to drag files from one window to another. If the two directories are on the same disk drive, then the operation will remove the files from their original directory after they've been copied to the new directory. If the two directories are on different disk drives, then the files will be preserved in the original directory. You can move files to another disk, even if you don't have a window open on that disk, by simply dragging a file to one of the disk drive icons. This is particularly useful for quickly copying a file to a floppy disk.

File Manager doesn't only know what files are stored on your disks, but it also dynamically tracks the file activities of all your Windows applications. For example, try the following. Use File Manager to display the C drive's root directory on one side of your screen, and open the Notepad utility on the other side of the screen. Type a line or two in the Notepad window, and then use its Save As command to save the file in the root directory. You should notice that File Manager instantly updates its display of the C root directory to show the new file. This is possible because Windows sends messages to notify File Manager of many file operations, such as file creation.

Besides file management, File Manager is also a useful utility for starting applications. If you double-click on most document files, File Manager will automatically try to find the application that works with that type of document, and then start that application. File Manager determines what application to use by looking at the three-letter extension of the document file, and by consulting the Windows registration database. An alternative way to use File Manager to start an application is to select a document in a File Manager window and then use the File-Run menu selection. Similarly, you can print documents by selecting them in a File Manager window and then using the File-Print menu selection.

How File Manager Works

When File Manager starts, it gets its initial window configuration from the WINFILE.INI file in the Windows directory.

WINFILE.INI

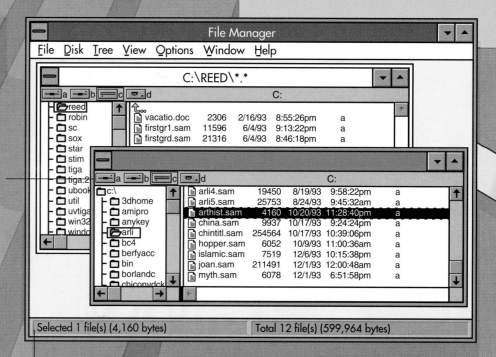

The disk icons at the top of each window let you switch from one disk drive to another. If you drag a file and drop it on a disk drive icon, you'll copy the file to that disk.

The status line shows information about selected files on the left, and it summarizes the current directory on the right.

File Manager lets you select multiple files. If you click on one file and then hold down the Shift key when you click on a second file, File Manager will select the two specified files, and all files in between them. If you hold down the Ctrl key while you select files, File Manager will let you select multiple individual files.

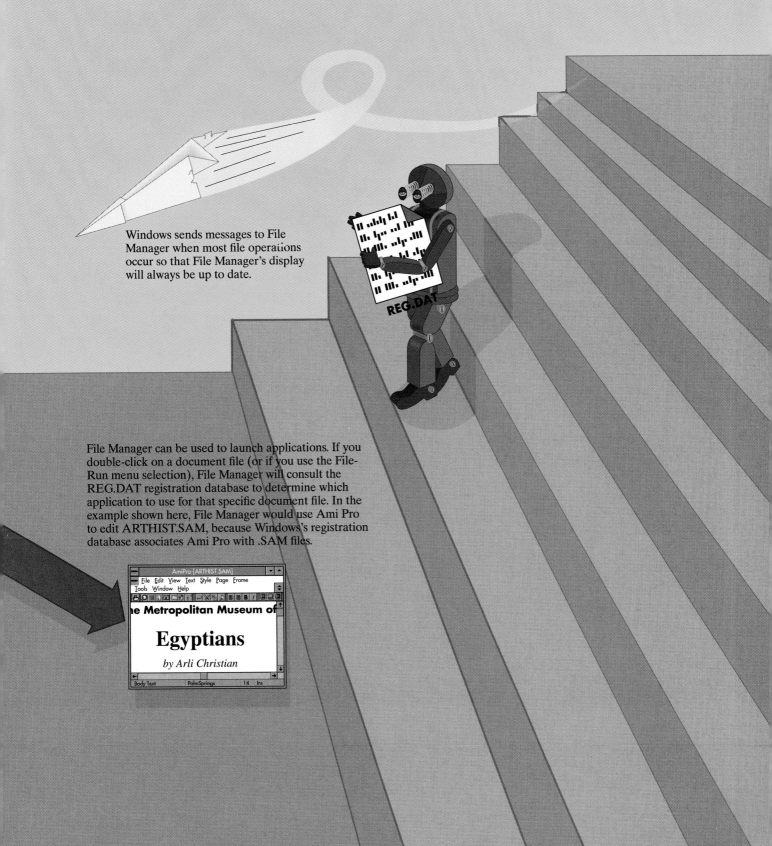

Windows sends messages to File Manager when most file operations occur so that File Manager's display will always be up to date.

REG.DAT

File Manager can be used to launch applications. If you double-click on a document file (or if you use the File-Run menu selection), File Manager will consult the REG.DAT registration database to determine which application to use for that specific document file. In the example shown here, File Manager would use Ami Pro to edit ARTHIST.SAM, because Windows's registration database associates Ami Pro with .SAM files.

AmiPro - [ARTHIST.SAM]

File Edit View Text Style Page Frame
Tools Window Help

The Metropolitan Museum of

Egyptians

by Arli Christian

Body Text   PalmSprings   14   Ins

How the Control Panel Works

THE WINDOWS CONTROL PANEL utility lets you customize your Windows system: specify your desktop colors, the sounds that are played when certain events occur, date and time formats, the sensitivity of your mouse, and so on. Some of these settings, such as your background wallpaper selection, are cosmetic, and others, such as the date format or the mouse sensitivity, help you tailor Windows so that it fits you like a glove.

When you launch the Control Panel utility, it displays a window that contains about a dozen icons. Each icon represents one Control Panel applet. An *applet* is just what it sounds like: a miniature utility. Each applet manages one group of settings. For example, the Color applet lets you specify the colors that are used in Windows, and the Fonts applet lets you specify what fonts will be loaded on your system.

Most of the Windows settings managed by Control Panel are stored in .INI files in the Windows System directory. For example, if you modify the mouse double-click speed using Control Panel, your new setting will be stored in the DoubleClickSpeed parameter in WIN.INI. You can always use a Windows text editor, such Notepad or SysEdit, to modify a setting directly, but why bother? When you use Control Panel to adjust the double-click speed, you can use a slider control to make the adjustment, and you can immediately test the settings to find the one that's best for you.

When Control Panel starts to execute, it automatically loads MAIN.CPL, which contains most of the Control Panel applets. Next, it looks for any installed Windows device drivers that include a Control Panel applet. Then, it looks in the file CPL.INI to determine the names of additional applets that should be loaded. In the last step, Windows looks in the Windows System directory for even more applets, which are identified by the .CPL filename extension. At this point Control Panel usually loads DRIVERS.CPL, SOUND.CPL, and CPWIN386.CPL, which contain the Drivers, Sound, and 386 Enhanced Control Panel applets. Once all the applets have been identified, Control Panel displays their icons and waits for you to select one by double-clicking on it.

Control Panel is an extensible application—it is designed so that hardware and software vendors can write their own Control Panel applets, which are automatically incorporated into the standard Control Panel main window. For example, the vendor of a network board might provide a Control Panel applet so that you could specify settings used by the network driver.

Another design feature of Control Panel is that applications can automatically start Control Panel applets. For example, a spreadsheet application could start Control Panel's Colors applet, so that you could choose a new set of system colors. Control Panel is built on the notion of flexibility; your copy of Windows can be as you like it.

How Control Panel Works

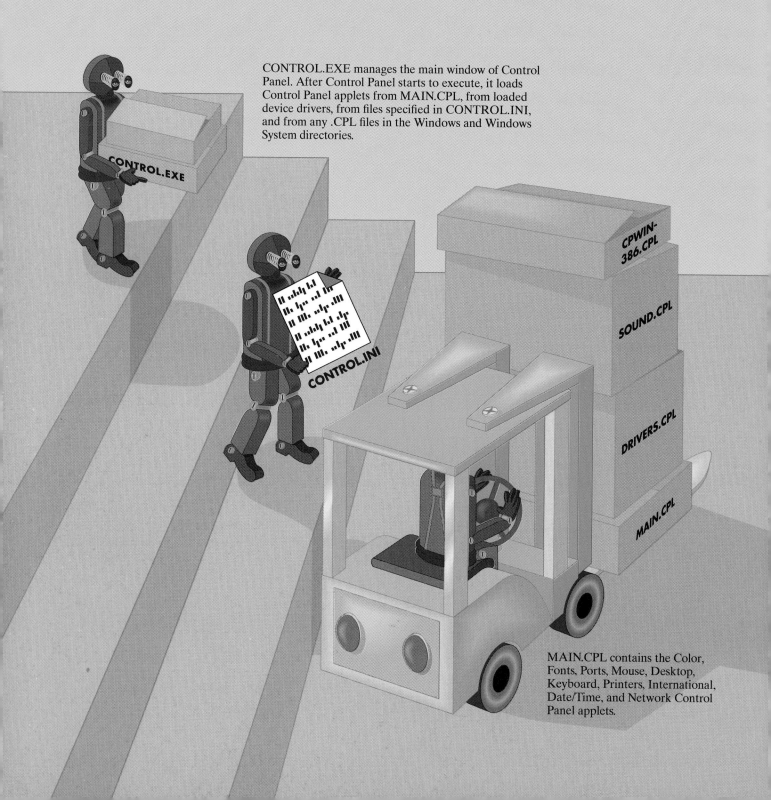

CONTROL.EXE manages the main window of Control Panel. After Control Panel starts to execute, it loads Control Panel applets from MAIN.CPL, from loaded device drivers, from files specified in CONTROL.INI, and from any .CPL files in the Windows and Windows System directories.

CONTROL.EXE

CONTROL.INI

CPWIN-386.CPL

SOUND.CPL

DRIVERS.CPL

MAIN.CPL

MAIN.CPL contains the Color, Fonts, Ports, Mouse, Desktop, Keyboard, Printers, International, Date/Time, and Network Control Panel applets.

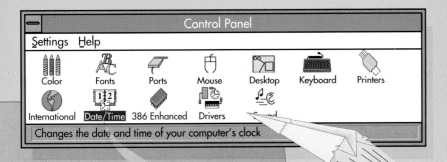

The main Control Panel window and the Control Panel applets communicate with each other using special Windows messages.

Most Control Panel applets save setting information in .INI files, often in WIN.INI. For example, the Mouse applet stores information about your mouse preferences in WIN.INI.

SwapMouseButtons = NO
DoubleClickSpeed = 350
MouseSpeed = 1

WIN.INI

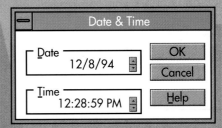

How Windows Help Works

ONE LITTLE-NOTICED area in which Windows excels is its help system. Yes, applications contained help systems long before Windows was a gleam in its developer's eyes. But those early help systems were unique to their application, and were generally limited compared with the help system that is now a standard part of most Windows applications.

Most Windows services are provided by the Windows kernel—that part of Windows loaded into memory during the boot process. For example, the graphics and text services described in Part 2 of this book are kernel services. In contrast, Windows's help service is provided by a Windows utility, which is called WinHelp.

There are three common ways to access help from within a Windows application: by pressing F1, by pressing a help button within a dialog box, or by using the Help menu. Once help has been selected in one of these three ways the application asks Windows to start the WinHelp utility. The application always tells WinHelp the name of the help file, and often supplies WinHelp with a context identifier that tells it which topic to display first.

During the next step, the WinHelp utility takes over. It opens the help file, and if a context identifier has been supplied, it immediately goes to the requested topic and displays it on the screen. If a specific topic hasn't been requested, then WinHelp starts by displaying the help file's table of contents on the screen. From this point forward, the help session is controlled interactively. When you're finished with WinHelp, you can close it by selecting File, then Exit, on the menu, or you can simply switch back to your application, leaving WinHelp running and ready for your next query.

WinHelp's main task is to interpret and display the information in a help file. Help files, whose names customarily have the .HLP suffix, contain three types of information: help, formatting, and control. Help information includes both text and graphics. It's the content that you view, and it's by far the largest component of most help files. Formatting information specifies the text typeface, type sizes, type style, graphics placement, and so on. This information is similar to the format information stored in most word processor document files. Control information includes many different facilities that provide WinHelp with its impressive abilities. For example, WinHelp provides a linking capability that lets you jump from one topic to another. The control information in help files differentiates the Windows help system from its anemic DOS predecessors. For example, with control information WinHelp can add buttons to its button bar, create additional windows to display help information, and allow for customization of WinHelp's menu. As you can see, WinHelp provides most of the features of a programming language.

Creating a help file is a job that's usually shared by software developers and documentation authors. In part, a help file is standard software documentation, and in part, it is a program that is best written by software developers. The first step in creating a help file is to create a word processor document that contains the text, graphics, and control information for the help file. Then, a Windows software development utility called the Help Compiler translates the help document into a help file. As in all software development, there is a cycle of testing, refinement, improvement, and recompilation that is repeated until the help system is complete.

WinHelp offers an annotation feature, which you can access by selecting Annotate from the Edit menu. When you select Annotate, you can type in a note that will be associated with the current page of help. In the future, when you access the same help page, a small paper-clip icon will appear at the top of the page, and you can click on the paper clip to see or change the annotation. Annotations are stored in .ANN files, usually in the Windows directory.

The most common function of WinHelp is to provide the help component of standard Windows applications. But for applications whose whole job is information presentation, WinHelp can be the entire application. For example, many information-rich applications are just collections of help files that you browse through in WinHelp. You may have used a WinHelp application without even realizing it.

How Windows Help Works

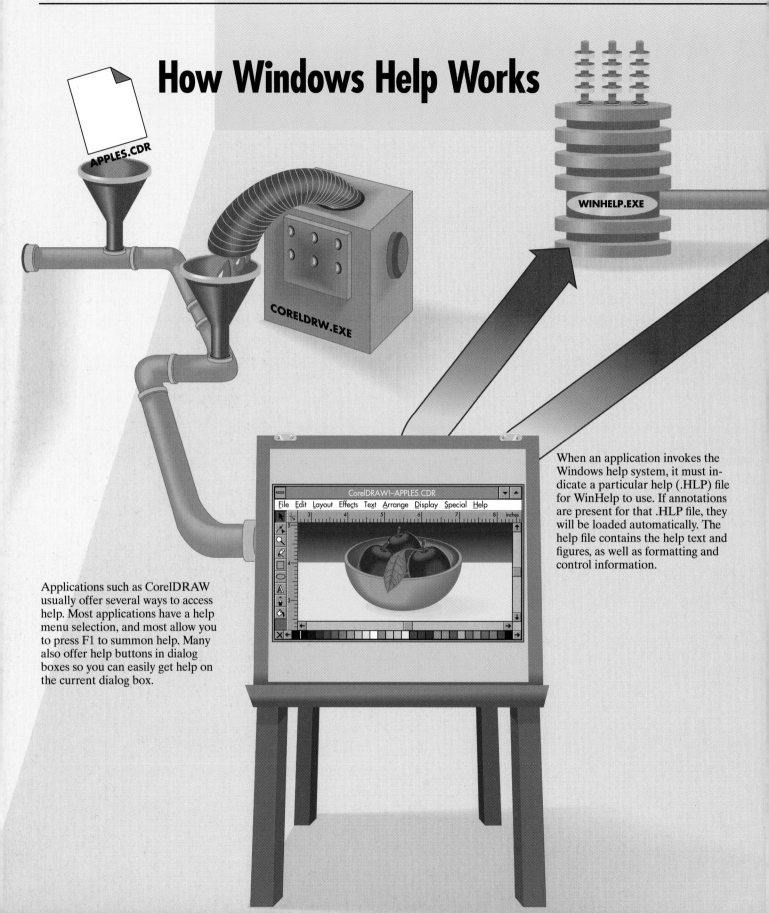

APPLES.CDR

CORELDRW.EXE

WINHELP.EXE

CorelDRAW!–APPLES.CDR

File Edit Layout Effects Text Arrange Display Special Help

Applications such as CorelDRAW usually offer several ways to access help. Most applications have a help menu selection, and most allow you to press F1 to summon help. Many also offer help buttons in dialog boxes so you can easily get help on the current dialog box.

When an application invokes the Windows help system, it must indicate a particular help (.HLP) file for WinHelp to use. If annotations are present for that .HLP file, they will be loaded automatically. The help file contains the help text and figures, as well as formatting and control information.

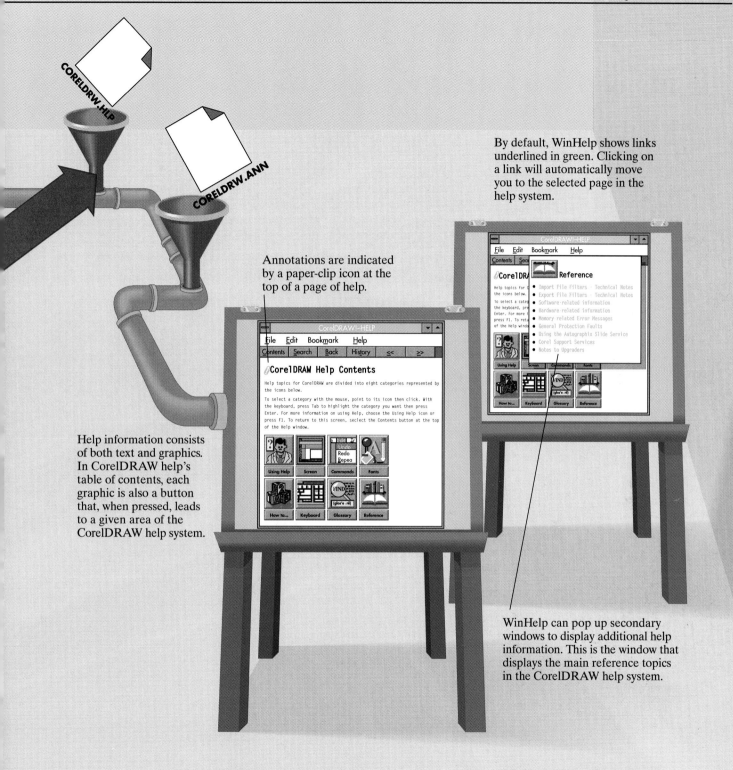

By default, WinHelp shows links underlined in green. Clicking on a link will automatically move you to the selected page in the help system.

Annotations are indicated by a paper-clip icon at the top of a page of help.

Help information consists of both text and graphics. In CorelDRAW help's table of contents, each graphic is also a button that, when pressed, leads to a given area of the CorelDRAW help system.

WinHelp can pop up secondary windows to display additional help information. This is the window that displays the main reference topics in the CorelDRAW help system.

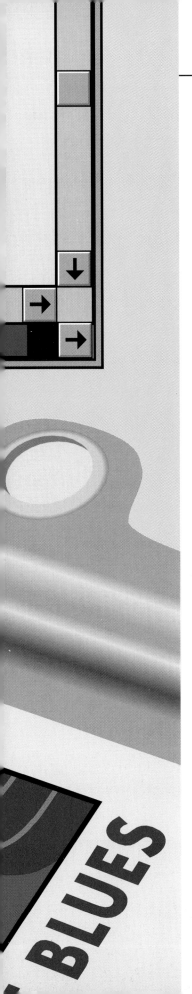

APPLICATION
TO
APPLICATION

4

CONTENTS

Chapter 14: How the Clipboard Works
102

Chapter 15: How Dynamic Data Exchange Works
108

Chapter 16: How Object Linking and Embedding Works
114

GREAT LITERATURE HAS often addressed the theme of relationships. For example, John Donne wrote that "No man is an island, entire of itself; every man is a piece of the continent, a part of the main…." A latter day Donne, addressing smaller concerns, might note that no Windows program is an island, entire of itself. Instead, Windows programs are written to work together, so each is a part of the main.

The quotation in the previous paragraph shows how Windows applications can work together. Of course, the quotation could have been researched in a traditional reference book. Instead, the quotation was found in Microsoft Bookshelf's version of *Bartlett's Quotations*. From Microsoft's CD-ROM version of Bartlett's, the quotation was copied to the Windows Clipboard, and then it was pasted into this document.

Microsoft Bookshelf wasn't specially written to work with word processors, but rather it was written to be a communicative, cooperative member of the Windows family. Like nearly all Windows applications, Bookshelf can work with the Windows Clipboard, which is analogous to a standard clipboard. Some applications, like Bookshelf, only use the Clipboard for either input or output, but most applications, like Ami Pro or Word, can copy information to the Clipboard, and paste information from the Clipboard.

A second application-to-application communication path in Windows is dynamic data exchange (DDE). DDE is like a pipe; it lets data flow from one application to another. For example, you might use DDE to connect a program reading stock prices over the phone line to a standard spreadsheet. As the prices change, the spreadsheet will automatically receive the new values.

Windows's newest communications technology is object linking and embedding (OLE). OLE allows several applications to manage a document cooperatively. Each application tends to its own data, so you're always using the best tool for the job. For example, in a financial report, your word processor would manage the text, your spreadsheet would tend to the numerical tables, your charting program would manage the graphs, and your clip-art program would provide the graphics.

It's important to understand how OLE is different from using the cut-and-paste feature to transfer data. Like OLE, the cut-and-paste feature lets you compose a document from bits and pieces supplied by separate applications. Cut and paste is both powerful and convenient, but it only provides a snapshot; once the paste operation is complete, you're done. With OLE, when you move your cursor to the table and double-click, the spreadsheet menus and environment appear; this lets you use the spreadsheet to interact with the spreadsheet data. If you move your cursor to a chart and double-click, your charting program takes over so that you can tune and tweak the chart.

Synergy is the key to using Windows productively. Working smoothly with several applications to produce a single document is not what you notice first when you sit down to use Windows, but this synergy is what stays with you over time, helping you manage your information.

CHAPTER
14

How the Clipboard Works

SYNERGY OF APPLICATIONS is the biggest advantage of Windows over DOS. But some-what surprisingly, it is one of the least heralded advantages. Synergy means you can create a spreadsheet using Lotus's 1-2-3 and then place that spreadsheet in a document that you're editing using WordPerfect. Synergy means that you can display a map of Ireland using DeLorme's Global Explorer, and then paste that map into a poster that you're drawing using CorelDRAW. Synergy means your applications work together.

The key to synergy is the Windows Clipboard, which allows applications to exchange text, graphics, and other information. The basic operation of the Clipboard is straightforward. When you select the Edit menu's Cut or Copy command in a Windows application, that application clears any current data in the Clipboard and then notifies the Clipboard that it has new information to manage. You can retrieve the contents of the Clipboard, using the original application or any others, by selecting the Paste command in the Edit menu. Applications aren't required to support cut and paste, but nearly all do. The application that copies something to the Clipboard is called the server, and the application that pastes in something from the Clipboard is called the client.

The Windows Clipboard is a service provided by Windows. It's not to be confused with the Clipboard Viewer utility, CLIPBRD.EXE, discussed later. The Clipboard Viewer is an ordinary utility that can interact with the Clipboard, as can most other Windows programs.

The term *clipboard* certainly suggests its function, but the Windows Clipboard is far more dynamic than a traditional clipboard. For example, the Windows Clipboard often has multiple data formats for whatever it contains. If you copy a graphic into the Clipboard, the server application will probably notify the Clipboard that it has several graphics formats available. This is somewhat like a real clipboard that is holding the same photographic image in three formats: a color print, a black-and-white print, and a 35mm transparency.

The Windows Clipboard often doesn't store the information. Instead, it is able to just keep track of which application is the server, and what formats are available. This is somewhat like a real clipboard that is holding a note, *the pictures are in the center desk drawer*, rather than the actual photos. Each time you copy information to the Clipboard, whatever it currently contains is discarded.

If an application tries to exit while it contains Clipboard information, the Clipboard will try to make its own copy. If Windows terminates while data is in the Clipboard, then that data will be lost.

The Clipboard service in Windows automatically supports many common text and graphics formats, including plain ASCII text, Windows bitmaps, Windows metafiles, and TIFF (Tag Image File Format, a common bitmap grahics format). Applications programs can also supply private data formats. For example, when CorelDRAW puts information into the Clipboard, it supplies a private data format called CorelMetafile in addition to other standard formats. Private data formats are used within an application or family of applications from a single vendor to implement cut and paste, but generally aren't used for cut and paste with applications from other vendors.

The Windows Clipboard was originally intended for relatively simple text and graphics exchange between pairs of cooperating, but not interacting, applications. Today, the Clipboard has been extended to include a role in object linking and embedding (OLE). OLE, which will be discussed further in Chapter 16, supports compound documents. In a compound document, several applications cooperate and interact, each managing a different type of data. For example, a financial report might include text, spreadsheets, and graphics, each managed by a different program. OLE transactions are usually initiated when the special OLE data formats Native, OwnerLink, and/or ObjectLink are placed in the Clipboard. Pasting one of these formats into a document initiates the OLE interaction, which then proceeds on its own.

You can use the Clipboard viewer utility to see what's available in the Windows Clipboard. The main window of the Clipboard automatically shows one of the formats in the Clipboard. You can use the Display menu to select one of the additional formats that is available. Formats that the Clipboard utility can't display, such as OLE and private data, are grayed in the Display menu.

How the Clipboard Works

The Windows Clipboard mimics a traditional clipboard. An application can copy information to the Clipboard, or paste in information from the Clipboard. Thus the Windows Clipboard provides a cut/paste capability within an application, and it provides an easy way for you to transfer text or graphics from one application to another.

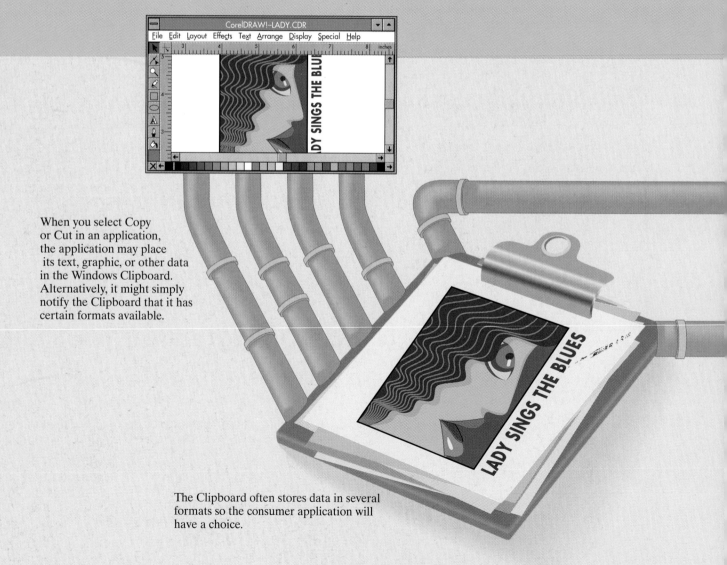

When you select Copy or Cut in an application, the application may place its text, graphic, or other data in the Windows Clipboard. Alternatively, it might simply notify the Clipboard that it has certain formats available.

The Clipboard often stores data in several formats so the consumer application will have a choice.

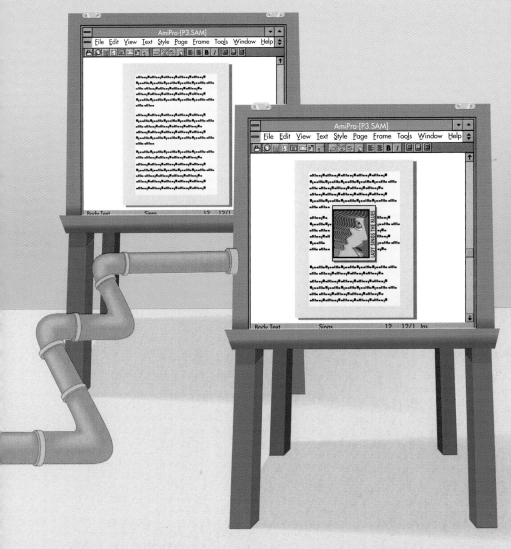

When you select Paste in an application, the application chooses a format from the Clipboard and inserts that format of the data into the document.

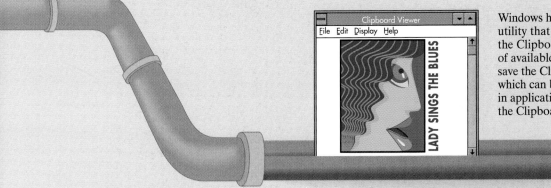

Windows has a Clipboard Viewer utility that lets you see what's in the Clipboard, along with the list of available formats. It also lets you save the Clipboard contents in a file, which can be useful for saving data in applications that can copy data to the Clipboard, but not to a file.

How Dynamic Data Exchange Works

DYNAMIC DATA EXCHANGE (DDE) creates a data pipeline from one Windows application to another. Unlike the Clipboard, which provides a data snapshot, DDE can support a continuous flow of information between two applications. If you want to create a chart in one program and use it in another, then the Clipboard is just the ticket. But if you want a chart or table that is updated continuously, then DDE is the right technology.

DDE servers produce data and place it in the pipeline, and DDE clients consume data, taking it out of the pipeline. For example, if you want a chart that continuously displays the temperatures for the last 24 hours, you need a DDE server application that can continuously measure the temperature, and you need a DDE client application that can produce graphs. DDE lets you create a data pipeline connecting two applications. This lets each application focus on its own task.

Before OLE (discussed in Chapter 16) was created, Windows only supported the Clipboard and DDE for data transfer. Thus, DDE was used then where OLE would be used today. For example, in the past, you might have used DDE to link a spreadsheet to a word processor. Whenever you changed the spreadsheet data, the corresponding table in your application would also change. Today such chores are usually handled by OLE, and DDE is commonly used for more automatic tasks such as monitoring stock prices and managing other live data.

DDE is implemented by a set of Windows messages that allow a pair of applications to create a DDE conversation. The client and server applications exchange DDE messages to arrange the data transfer. The DDE messages go back and forth between the two applications, but data flows only from server to client.

There are three types of DDE pipelines that applications can create: *cold*, which means the data is updated only at the client's request; *warm*, which means the server notifies the client when new data is available; and *hot*, which means the server sends new data as it becomes available.

DDE transactions can be initiated by either the client or the server. The easiest way is to start the transaction from the server. If you're using a program that can function as a DDE server, simply select some data and then select Copy. The application will, as usual, place multiple data formats into the Clipboard, including the special format called Link that signifies the ability to perform a

DDE transaction. Then you can use the Paste Special or Paste Link command from the Edit menu of the DDE-capable client to paste in the DDE link. From that point forward, the DDE transaction proceeds without further use of the Clipboard or additional user intervention.

DDE transactions can also be initiated by the client. When a client initiates a DDE transaction, it must identify the DDE server that it wants to use and the data that it wants to acquire. DDE data is identified using a triplet that consists of an application name, a topic name, and an item name. The format of the triplet is APPNAME|TOPIC!ITEM. For example, if you want to use DDE to place temperature data from oven number 3 at a bakery into a spreadsheet, you would place the triplet TEMPSERV|OVENS!3 into a cell of the spreadsheet. This example assumes that your machine has an application called TEMPSERV.EXE that is monitoring temperatures, and that it supports a topic called OVENS and an item called 3. If you want to acquire IBM's stock prices, the DDE triplet might be TICKER|NYSE!IBM, which assumes a stock quote program named TICKER.EXE, which supports a topic called NYSE, and an item called IBM.

Many DDE servers support a topic called SYSTEM that provides a list of all the topics that the server offers. This lets the client interrogate the server to see what is available and then place that information into a convenient menu or dialog box so that topics can be selected from a list, rather than looked up in a reference.

The newest wrinkle in DDE technology is network DDE. Network DDE allows applications to exchange data using a DDE pipeline even if they are on separate machines. Network DDE is part of Windows for Workgroups, but is not a part of standard Windows 3.1.

How DDE Works

DDE Links: Cold means data flows only at the client's request; warm means client is notified when data is available; hot means client receives data whenever it is available.

Windows for Workgroups allows DDE transactions to occur over a network. This lets you create a DDE link with a program that isn't running on your own PC.

Windows DDE creates a data pipeline between two Windows programs. The applications send messages to each other to coordinate the transfer, but data always flows from the server to the client.

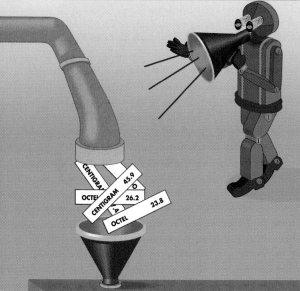

Windows provides the environment in which DDE can occur, but once the transfer starts, the two applications interact directly.

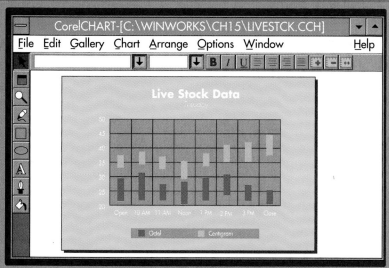

How Object Linking and Embedding Works

OBJECT LINKING AND EMBEDDING (OLE) is the newest technology in Windows. It supercharges the already powerful Clipboard and DDE technologies, to create a customized environment for working with information. OLE is a set of standards that allows you to create automatically updated links between documents. OLE breaks down the barriers between applications, allowing you to move seamlessly from one application to another while working on a single document.

OLE enables compound documents—containers for other documents—which are multipart documents that are composed using several applications programs. If a compound document contains a spreadsheet document, then the spreadsheet (or a portion of the spreadsheet) is stored in its own container. The application that manages the overall document, often a word processor, doesn't need to know how to work with the spreadsheet data; all it needs to know is the name of the spreadsheet application. When the spreadsheet needs to be displayed or edited, the spreadsheet container is passed to the spreadsheet application, which does all the work.

What's most impressive about OLE is that it works seamlessly. Simply by moving the cursor from one area of a document to another and double-clicking, you automatically switch from one application to another. Menus, toolbars, and the like, all change automatically, adapting to whatever task you are addressing.

Let's look at the terms *object*, *linking*, and *embedding*, because each is a key to understanding OLE technology. In the OLE lexicon, *object* refers to a marriage of information and behavior. For example, an OLE object might be a graphic that can be edited, a table that can be manipulated using a spreadsheet, or a paragraph that can be formatted using a word processor. If you copy a static image onto the Clipboard, it's just that, an image; by itself it's not an object because it can't be modified. If an OLE-capable application places an image object onto the Clipboard, then that application, which is called an OLE server, can continue to modify and shape the image. And remember that the Clipboard supports multiple formats simultaneously (see Chapter 14). When you paste, say, an image into the Clipboard, an OLE server application will usually place standard image formats in the Clipboard for use by any application, including those that don't support OLE.

Plus the server will place object versions of the image in the Clipboard for applications that can receive OLE objects, which are called OLE clients. In the client, selecting Paste will usually insert a plain image; you typically use Paste Special or Insert Object to insert an OLE object.

Linking and embedding are the two remaining concepts in OLE. Both terms specify where the data in an object is stored. When data is linked, the compound document doesn't actually contain the object (image, text, spreadsheet), but instead knows where to find it. This means that there is only one copy of the data. The alternative is object embedding, in which a copy of the original data is placed in the compound document. When an object is embedded there are two copies; changes to the embedded object don't alter the original, and vice versa.

Each OLE object supports a set of operations, which are called verbs. For example, a video or audio clip might support the verbs Play and Rewind, and an image might support the verbs Display and Edit. A client application can query an OLE object to find out what verbs it supports.

OLE also lets one application control another, which is called OLE automation. This lets you use a programming language such as Visual Basic or Realizer to automate a routine task. For example, you could use OLE automation to load a set of weekly expense reports into a spreadsheet and then calculate totals. You would specify the outline of the task using, say, the Visual Basic programming language. Visual Basic would then use OLE automation to direct, for example, the Quattro Pro spreadsheet to perform the calculations. OLE automation lets you use your applications as building blocks when constructing customized information-management systems.

OLE is implemented using the Clipboard and DDE for mortar and bricks. Like DDE conversations, OLE conversations are implemented by exchanging Windows messages. These messages enable applications to negotiate the details of how they will cooperate. But in OLE, the negotiation goes far beyond what data will be transferred and includes topics such as managing menus, querying objects to discover their actions (verbs), displaying toolbars and status bars, and displaying OLE objects.

OLE interactions are usually started when an OLE server places either the OwnerLink or ObjectLink format in the Clipboard. OwnerLink means the server can supply an embedded object; ObjectLink means that a linked object is available. Then you would use the client application to paste one of these formats into your document. Pasting the OwnerLink or ObjectLink format into a document creates a container inside the document to house the OLE object. The server continues to be responsible for display, editing, and so on, of the object; the client only has to store the object's data (embedding) or remember where the data is stored (linking). When you start to interact with the object, the client application hands control to the server. When you're through working with the object, the server returns control to the client application.

How OLE Works

You usually place an OLE object into a document using the Paste Special or Insert Object menu selection. This operation initiates the OLE link between the two applications. After inserting the object, the applications communicate by sending each other Windows messages.

You often initiate an OLE operation by copying an existing object to the Clipboard using an OLE server application. (The alternative is to use the Insert New Object command from within an OLE client.)

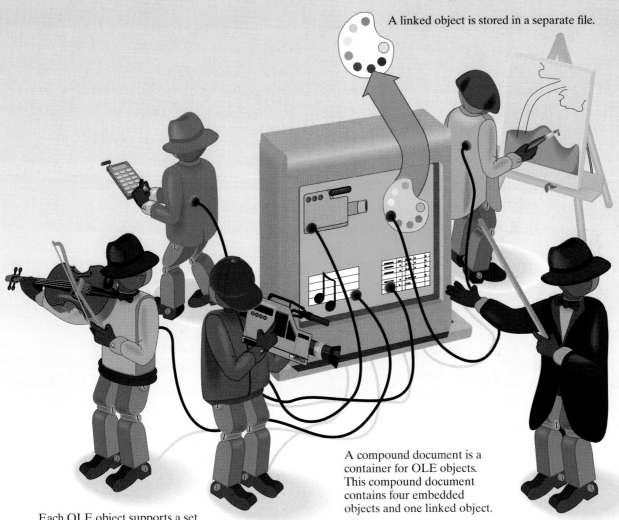

A linked object is stored in a separate file.

A compound document is a container for OLE objects. This compound document contains four embedded objects and one linked object.

Each OLE object supports a set of operations, which are called verbs because they are actions. For example, audio and video-clip objects usually support the Play, Stop, and Rewind verbs.

A compound document is managed by an OLE client application. The client only has to store the data, letting the object's server provide the object's operations.

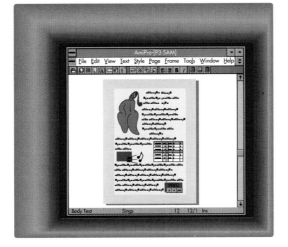

OLE works behind the scenes to display a compound document. The client application calls on servers, as necessary, to display and manage their parts of a document.

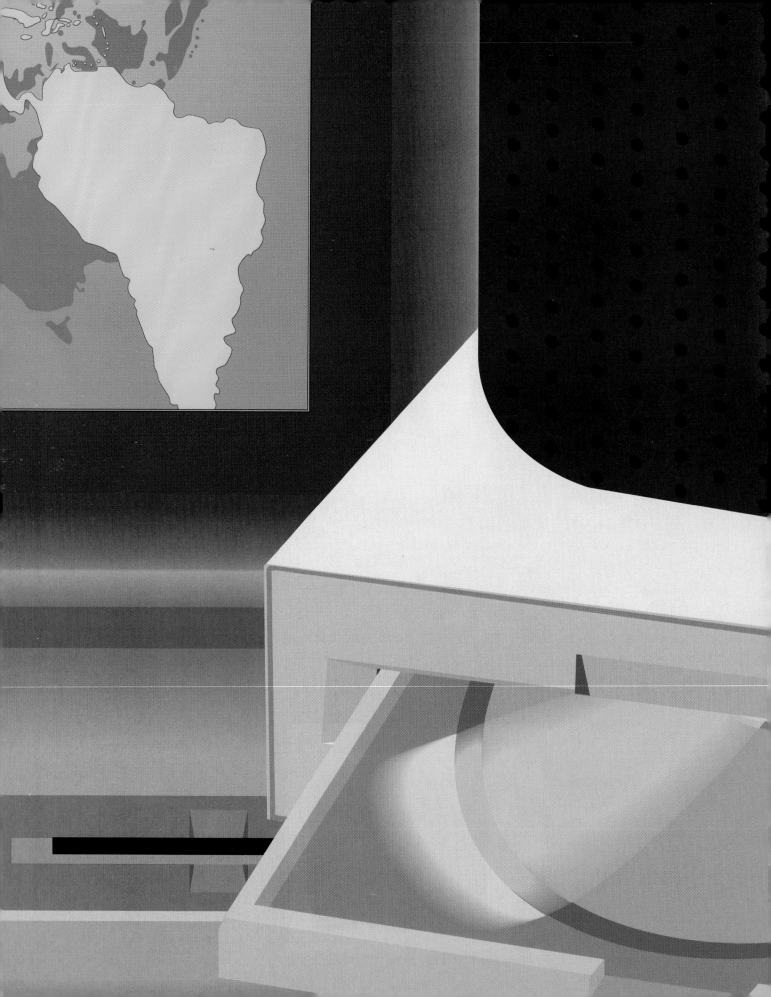

THE MULTIMEDIA EXPERIENCE

CONTENTS

Chapter 17: How Windows Makes Sounds
124

Chapter 18: How Windows Plays Video Clips
130

Chapter 19: How Animation Works
136

OVERVIEW

WINDOWS IS FAST becoming a means of mass communication. The keys to this emerging ability are Windows's newfound prowess with sound and video. Of course, it also takes hardware to make it work, but increasing numbers of computers are being sold with multimedia hardware. Traditional desktop productivity applications, such as word processors and spreadsheets, are starting to make some use of multimedia, but the real breakthroughs are in the fields of entertainment and education, which rely on multimedia for their message.

Multimedia capabilities were first delivered in the era of Windows 3.0 by Microsoft's Multimedia Extensions, which primarily added audio to the Windows repertoire. The Multimedia Extensions became a standard part of Windows in version 3.1. To make use of the Multimedia Extensions you need an audio board, such as Creative Labs's Sound Blaster, plus speakers or headphones and a microphone for audio input.

To display a movie, the only hardware you need is a good video adapter and a software driver. Applications that display video clips in Windows 3.1 usually provide a standard driver for displaying video movies, such as Microsoft's Video for Windows. Future versions of Windows will likely incorporate drivers for displaying video movies, making Windows a truly multimedia system. Video input is also possible, but you need a relatively expensive video capture board and a very fast computer.

CD-ROM is an important component of multimedia, because audio and video clips have voracious appetites for storage space. Lincoln's Gettysburg address in text requires about 1,500 (75 score) bytes of storage, as a 2-minute audio clip, it requires about 1.3 megabytes of storage, and as a 2-minute video clip, it requires about 18 megabytes of storage. Numbers like these explain why multimedia-capable PCs need CD-ROM drives.

Multimedia capacity is important to Windows because it allows the computer to encompass other media. But of course there's an advantage—the computer is interactive while other media are passive. For example, when you're playing an adventure game on your computer, you are constantly making choices and directing the action. When you're watching an action film on TV, you're a passive viewer, with no ability to influence the action. The computer is an individual media; that is, you can choose your own software and follow your own interests. But with TV and radio programs, you are limited to what is available at any given time—the networks, which are geared toward producing programs for the largest possible audience, determine the programs.

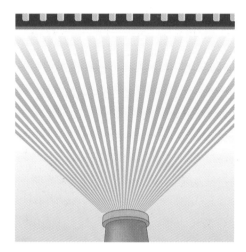

How Windows Makes Sounds

WINDOWS MAKES SOUNDS much as you do. When you're using your voice, whether speaking, singing, or shouting, your vocal cords are vibrating to shape, instant by instant, the sound that you are making. Similarly, Windows can produce sounds by specifying, instant by instant, the sound wave that should be produced by the speaker. This capability is called waveform audio because it works by recording the shape of the sound wave.

Windows is able to use the PC's speaker for waveform output, but the results are rarely satisfactory for anything other than tones and chirps. For acceptable sound output, you need a sound board and a pair of speakers or headphones, and for recording sound, you need a microphone or other sound source. The waveform part of an audio board contains a high-speed interface to the PC bus, so that it can rapidly access sample data stored in main memory. It also contains a digital-to-analog conversion device, so that the digital information in the .WAV files can be converted to analog. Most audio boards also contain a digitizer, so that input from a microphone or other source can be converted to digital format and stored in a file.

Sound waveforms are customarily stored in .WAV files. The numbers in the file, called samples, record the exact shape of the sound waveform. When the waveform is played, Windows sends each digital value in the file to the sound board, which converts it to an analog waveform that is amplified and sent directly to the speaker. Several different formats are available, depending on the quality that is required. The most common format, which is adequate for voice reproduction, is to use 11,000 eight-bit samples to specify each second of sound. More samples per second, usually 22,000 or 44,000, allow reproduction of higher frequencies. Using 16-bit samples instead of 8-bit samples yields higher quality. You can filter or edit a waveform by using, for example, Microsoft's Multimedia Development Kit utility WaveEdit.

You can also make sound using an instrument. For example, with a piano, you can strike a key to produce a rich, complex sound. The keystroke starts the sound, and if you're a good pianist, the keystroke can subtly shape and enrich the sound. Mostly, though, the piano produces the tone on its own. Windows has much the same ability. It can instruct your sound board to produce, say, a middle-C piano note, or an A-sharp trumpet note, and then the sound board will tend to the details and output the note. This form of Windows sound production is called MIDI audio, because Windows makes use of a music industry standard—the musical instrument digital interface—to specify the sound.

MIDI has been in wide use in the music industry since the early eighties. It is used to connect keyboards and other control devices to synthesizers, drum machines, and other electronic sound-making machines. The MIDI portion of PC audio boards usually contains a basic synthesizer, plus connectors that you can use to hook up your PC to external MIDI devices, such as keyboards and sophisticated synthesizers.

MIDI sounds are usually stored in .MID files (or sometimes .RMI or .XMI files). MIDI files store events, such as Note On or Note Off. Windows sends the events in a .MID file to the audio board, which carries them out. For example, when the audio board receives a Note On command, it looks up the shape of the note in its own memory, much as if it had an onboard .WAV file describing the note's shape. Then the audio board, still acting on its own, converts the note description to analog to drive the speaker. MIDI files are much more compact than .WAV files, because it takes much less space to specify note start and stop times than it does to specify the detailed descriptions of sounds that are found in .WAV files.

You can produce sound by playing recorded sounds, too, such as audio CDs. Yes, Windows can even do that. Some CD-ROM software titles include sound recorded directly on the CD, which Windows plays back by telling the CD-ROM to move to a specific track and then play. You can listen to this audio feature by plugging headphones or speakers directly into the headphone jack on your computer's CD-ROM drive, but a more convenient solution is to connect the audio output of the CD-ROM drive to the mixer input on your audio board, so that a single pair of speakers attached to your audio board is used by all three sound sources. This connection is factory installed in most multimedia PCs, but you may have to make the connection yourself if you add multimedia components to an existing machine, or if you upgrade your sound board or CD-ROM drive on a multimedia machine.

How Windows Makes Sounds

A sound board for a multimedia PC must have an internal MIDI synthesizer. At minimum, the synthesizer must have three independent voices. Each voice must support at least a 6-note polyphony, which means the voice can contain six different notes at once.

Multimedia PCs must have a plug-in audio board (or equivalent circuitry on the motherboard) for producing sound.

AUDIO BOARD

MIDI SYNTHESIZER

DIGITAL TO ANALOG

AUDIO MIXER

The waveform section of an audio board converts the samples in .WAV files to analog. It needs a high-speed pathway to the PC data bus in order to play sounds without interruption.

WAVEFORM AUDIO

DIGITAL TO ANALOG

ANALOG TO DIGITAL

Like most disk controllers and display adapters, audio boards plug into the PC's data bus. This gives them a high-speed connection to the computer's CPU and memory.

CD-ROM

CD-ROMs can have data tracks, which contain data files, and audio tracks, which contain ordinary CD audio information. The CD-ROM in your PC has an audio out that can be connected to your sound board, so you can play audio tracks using the speakers connected to your sound board. Most CD-ROM drives also have a front-panel headphone jack for listening to CD-ROM audio.

Windows contains driver software for each type of audio board. The driver software communicates with the board via the PC data bus.

.WAV FILES

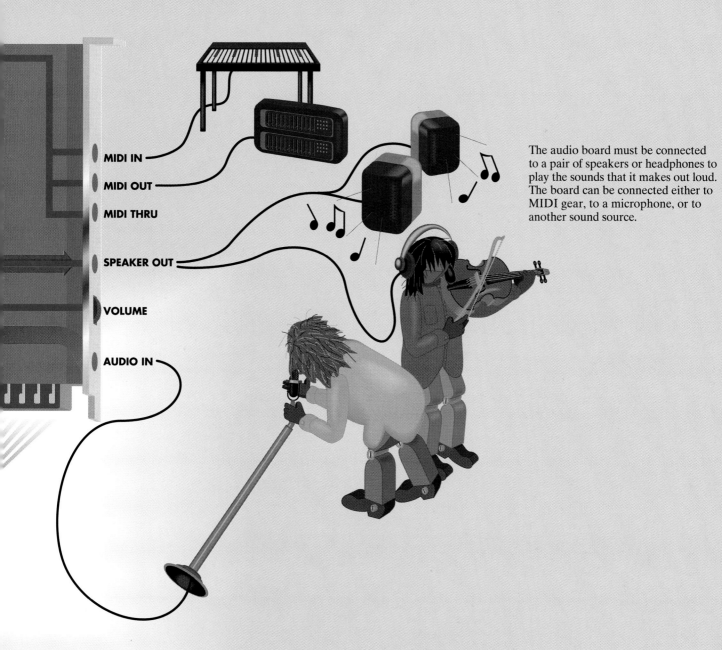

MIDI IN

MIDI OUT

MIDI THRU

SPEAKER OUT

VOLUME

AUDIO IN

The audio board must be connected
to a pair of speakers or headphones to
play the sounds that it makes out loud.
The board can be connected either to
MIDI gear, to a microphone, or to
another sound source.

How Windows Plays Video Clips

THE INVENTION AND evolution of video are defining events of the latter half of this century. In just 50 years, we've gone from a grainy, expensive, exclusive, black-and-white medium to a full-color, high quality, cheap, and universal medium. Video breakthroughs are occurring on several fronts, but perhaps the most exciting aspect is video's increasing role in desktop computing.

Digital video on the desktop is possible because performance of computers and display hardware is now adequate for video and there is increased storage capacity. Yes, hard disks are cheaper, bigger, and better every year. But more importantly, CD-ROMs have become widely available in the past few years, and CD-ROM is the home of most digital video clips.

You don't need any specialized equipment, other than a fast PC, to play prerecorded video clips. A CD-ROM is useful, because most video clips take up huge amounts of room, but any fast, modern PC with a color display will do. So if hardware isn't required, then what is the essence of desktop video technology? The answer: a good codec.

A *codec* (*COmpression/DECompression*) is a system for video compression and decompression. During image capture, the codec compresses the video data, so the data takes less space and can be accessed more rapidly. During playback, the codec must continually decompress the video to restore the original image. Without compression, PCs can't handle the load; it would be like trying to pour a gallon of liquid into a teaspoon. A single frame of video in digital form requires, at highest quality, about 1 megabyte of storage. Thirty such frames, which is just one second of motion video, take about 30 megabytes of storage. Or a minute? That requires 1.8 gigabytes on your hard disk. These numbers could be reduced somewhat by storing less information for each frame, but such simple techniques don't come close to solving the problem.

So to be practical, desktop video files must be compressed, heavily compressed. When spreadsheets or other document files are compressed, it's important that nothing be lost in the process; the decompression must exactly re-create the original file, which is called lossless compression. Imagine your distress if you decompressed a spreadsheet file and discovered that your figures had changed. But with images and sound, compression needn't be perfect, which is called lossy compression; what matters is that the decompressed image or sound closely resemble the original.

We'll accept a bit of background noise in a sound clip, or a slight loss of detail in a video clip, in exchange for a high compression ratio that allows many more sounds or pictures to be stored in a given space. Also, most compression systems allow trade-offs to be made between color fidelity, spatial resolution, and frame rates, so that different needs can be accommodated.

To create video clips, a camera or video tape recorder is attached to an image-capture board on the PC. The capture board converts the video signal to digital form, which is called digitization, and then the video is heavily compressed and stored in an .AVI file. *AVI* stands for *audio video interleaved,* and an .AVI file is just that, a series of audio and video segments together with timing information. During playback, Windows retrieves both sound and video from the file, using the file's timing information to keep them in sync. The sound is routed to the audio board, while the video is decompressed and displayed on the screen.

There is a wide performance range in computers running Windows, therefore codecs need to adapt to the playback environment. On slower computers, codecs must display fewer frames per second in smaller areas of the screen. For example, a low-end 386 PC might play video clips in a 160-by-120 window at 10 frames per second, and a high-end machine would be able to play the video in a 640-by-480 window at 20 or more frames per second. Sure, we'd all prefer the high end, but it's important for a codec to work acceptably well on all Windows systems.

How Windows Plays Video Clips

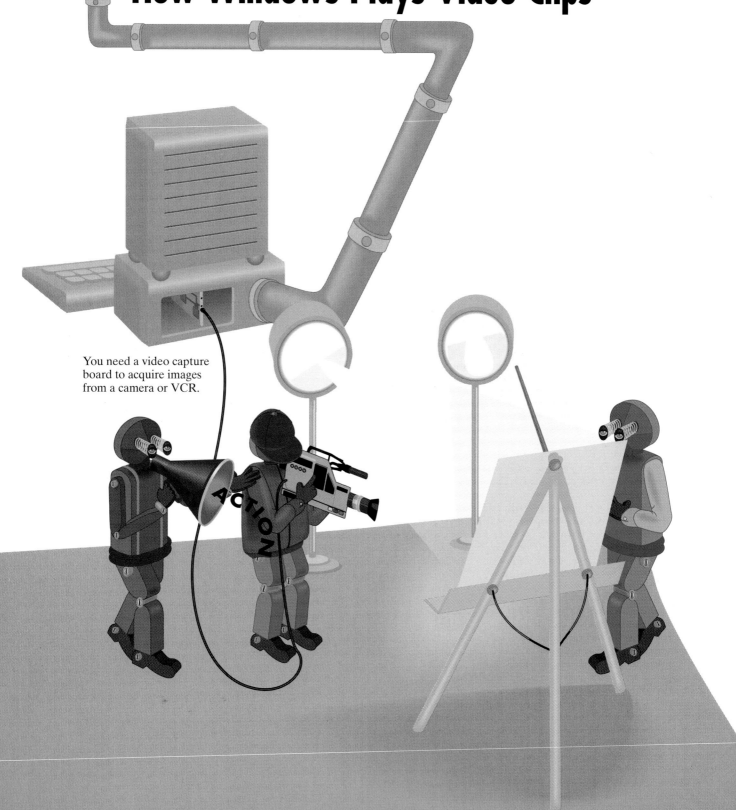

You need a video capture board to acquire images from a camera or VCR.

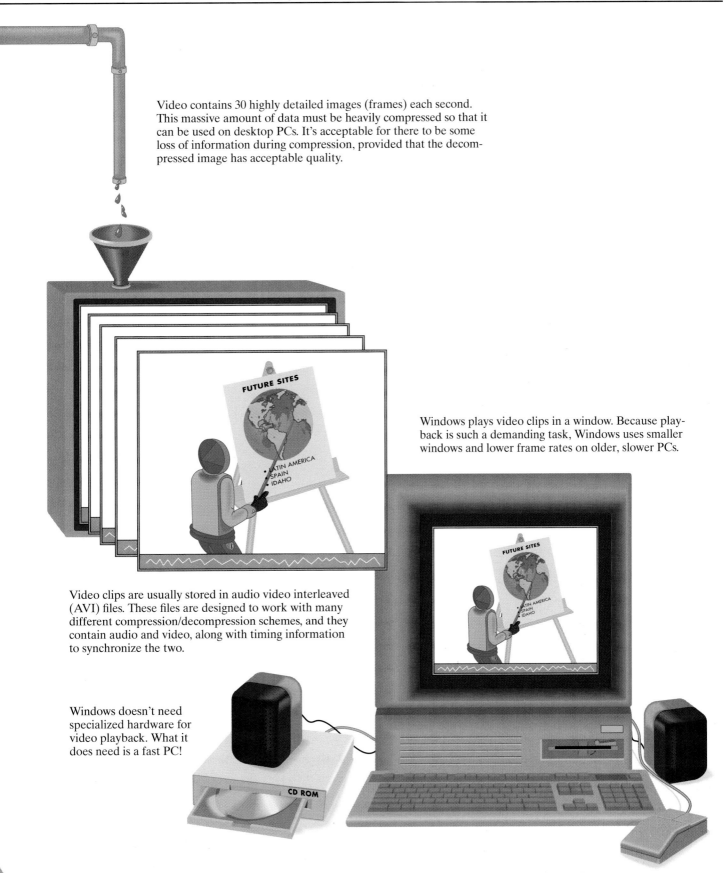

Video contains 30 highly detailed images (frames) each second. This massive amount of data must be heavily compressed so that it can be used on desktop PCs. It's acceptable for there to be some loss of information during compression, provided that the decompressed image has acceptable quality.

Windows plays video clips in a window. Because playback is such a demanding task, Windows uses smaller windows and lower frame rates on older, slower PCs.

Video clips are usually stored in audio video interleaved (AVI) files. These files are designed to work with many different compression/decompression schemes, and they contain audio and video, along with timing information to synchronize the two.

Windows doesn't need specialized hardware for video playback. What it does need is a fast PC!

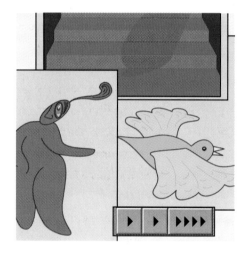

How Animation Works

NIMATION IS AN engaging way to present information. Animation is often associated with children's entertainment, and it's true that much Windows animation occurs in games and other software titles for children. Animation can also play a role in almost any software that delivers information, from a CD-ROM encyclopedia to software that offers home-repair tips.

Traditional film animation is based on drawings and paintings. First, a background image for the scene is created. Then, each character in the scene is painted onto an individual transparent celluloid sheet, or *cel*. The cels are stacked on top of the background painting and photographed to produce just one frame of the movie. Next, new cels are drawn for any character that moves, one new cel for each movement. Again, cels are layered on top of the background painting and photographed to produce every subsequent frame. This laborious process is repeated for every frame of the entire movie.

Windows contains animation facilities that duplicate the traditional process. No special hardware is needed, although animation works better on faster PCs with speedy displays.

Animated movies are created using multimedia authoring software. Typical authoring software lets you create or import the individual elements and then animate them. For things that change shape or appearance, you can specify a series of images. For example, to show a door opening, you would need three images of a door: closed, half open, and open. By changing images from closed to half open to open, you can create the impression of a door opening. And to create the image of a cloud drifting lazily across the sky, for example, you would specify the starting and ending positions of the cloud and the duration of the movement.

Many animation movements require both a sequence of images and a path over which the sequence is displayed. For example, an animation of a cat jumping off of a table would require a series of images of the cat in all the phases of jumping, plus the images would be placed on a path over a period of time. During playback, the cat's image would both change and move along a path during the animated jump.

The main component that Windows needs to play back an animation is a playback driver. A *playback driver* uses the images and instructions in a movie file to create an animation. Windows is designed to work with many different animation playback drivers. This allows vendors to create their own animation systems. For example, one vendor's animation system might be good for cartoon-style animation, and another might be preferred for animating technical drawings. When a program asks Windows to play an animation, it must tell Windows which movie playback driver to use, as well as what movie file to play.

The playback driver must keep track of what's in the foreground and what's in the background, because all of its drawing chores are based on what is on top of what. Just as importantly, the playback driver must keep track of what has changed so it can draw as little as possible. The driver also must restore whatever was underneath when top images move or change. Plus the playback driver must maintain synchronization with audio, attend to mouse clicks, and process other input. It's a lot of work and it must be performed quickly, or the animation will look jerky.

How Animation Works

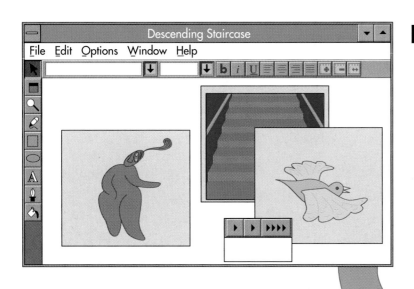

1 Animated digital movies are created using an *authoring* program, which brings together all the elements and lets you specify how each element moves or changes.

2 Authoring program output is placed into a movie file.

3 A movie file contains all the elements of a movie, together with instructions that specify the movements. Movie files are highly optimized so they can be processed rapidly during playback.

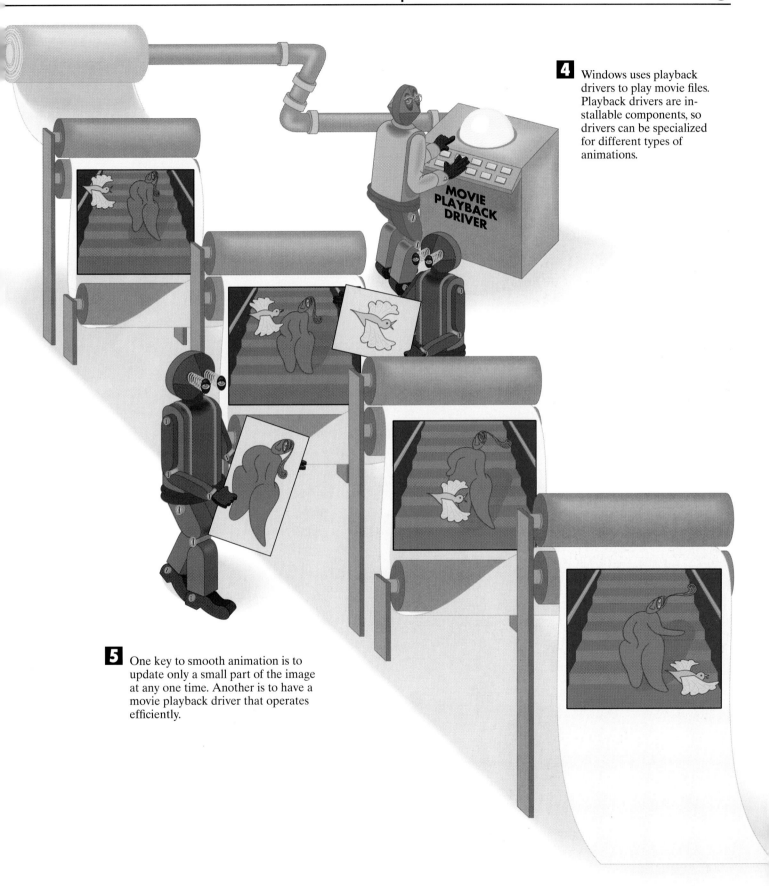

4 Windows uses playback drivers to play movie files. Playback drivers are installable components, so drivers can be specialized for different types of animations.

MOVIE PLAYBACK DRIVER

5 One key to smooth animation is to update only a small part of the image at any one time. Another is to have a movie playback driver that operates efficiently.

BEHIND THE SCENES

CONTENTS

Chapter 20: How Messages Work
146

Chapter 21: How DLLs Work
152

Chapter 22: How Virtual Memory Works
158

Chapter 23: How Input and Output Device Drivers Work
164

OVERVIEW

COMPLEX SYSTEMS such as Windows usually have both a visible part and a hidden part. If you want to understand a complex system, the visible part is the obvious place to start. But real understanding requires peeling away the outer layers so you can examine what's underneath. For example, you can't understand how a cuckoo clock works without taking off the case and examining its gears and levers. Similarly, you can't really understand Windows unless you look at how the hidden part works.

Previous sections of this book have covered aspects of Windows that are easily visible on the outside. All of these topics lead quickly to the interior terrain of Windows, so there has been a partial view of the interior in each discussion. But in this section of the book, the focus is on the interior.

The most prominent feature of the Windows landscape is messages. Most tasks in Windows are based on sending messages, a trait that sets Windows apart from older systems such as DOS. Perhaps its second most remarkable feature is its ability to add and subtract components while it is running. Windows is like a factory that adds on a new assembly line when demand soars, and then disassembles the new line when demand falls off. This remarkable ability is based on dynamic link libraries, or DLLs, which are discussed in Chapter 21.

Another prominent feature of the Windows landscape is virtual memory, which allows Windows to behave as if your PC had more memory than is actually installed. Virtual memory gives Windows the flexibility that's required to operate one application or many, whether on a machine with memory to spare, or one with memory shortages.

How Windows handles input and output hardware is also covered in this section. All computer systems have to work with keyboards, screens, and other I/O devices; such hardware is what makes it possible for us to interact with computers. Unlike most older computer systems, Windows provides full graphics support for most output devices, and it uses messages as part of its input device management. Both features help Windows create a supportive user interface.

How Messages Work

N WINDOWS, a *message* is a small packet of information that is sent to a window. For example, when you click the left mouse button, the window underneath the mouse pointer gets a "left mouse button clicked" message. The message provides the window with the mouse's location at the time of the click and the state of the Shift and Control keys. (The Shift and Control key states are provided to enable applications to differentiate between plain clicks, shift clicks, and control clicks.)

Messages are the heart of the Windows programming environment. They allow you to be in charge; whatever you do using the mouse or keyboard is translated into a message and routed to the appropriate window. When the window receives a message, it does whatever it needs to do. For example, if you click the mouse in a spreadsheet window, you'll probably select a cell; if you click the mouse in a word processor window you'll probably move the insertion point to the mouse pointer's position.

Windows applications are designed to be reactive. Applications must be prepared for all the possibilities, at any time and in any order. This gives you the freedom to make selections, enter text, use menus, use scroll bars, and so on, in your own way. Software written in environments that aren't message-based can attain the same flexibility, but it is much harder to do.

Each application contains a message queue. A *message queue* is simply a waiting line, like that at the box office outside a popular movie. When messages arrive they are placed onto the tail end of the queue. When messages are processed, they are removed from the head of the queue and the other messages move up.

Most messages are placed in an application message queue by Windows, and then the application takes them out and sends them directly to the appropriate window. A queue gives an application much-needed message-handling flexibility. For example, the application can use the queue as a filter and discard messages that it doesn't want to pass on to one of its windows. For example, an application can temporarily ignore keyboard input by simply discarding the keyboard messages from the queue.

Message queues also provide timing flexibility. Because the queue can store several messages, Windows needn't wait for the application to finish processing the current message before sending it another. Without the queue, Windows would be forced to operate in a more rigid, step-by-step manner.

Message queues differentiate between high-priority and low-priority messages. Low-priority messages politely stay at the end of the queue, letting high-priority messages pass to the front. The major use of this is to defer screen redrawing. This is important because screen redraw messages are often followed immediately by messages that modify the area that's just been redrawn. By deferring redraw until there are no other messages to process, Windows minimizes time spent drawing, which is usually time consuming.

Most window-management messages bypass the message queue and go directly to the target window. This ensures that the target window receives the message as quickly as possible, and it guarantees delivery.

How Messages Work

Each application has a message queue, which stores pending messages. High-priority messages, which are the most common type, are conveyed in order to the front of the queue and then routed by the application to one of its windows. Low-priority messages, such as the timer-expired message and the redraw message, are processed when there are no high-priority messages to process.

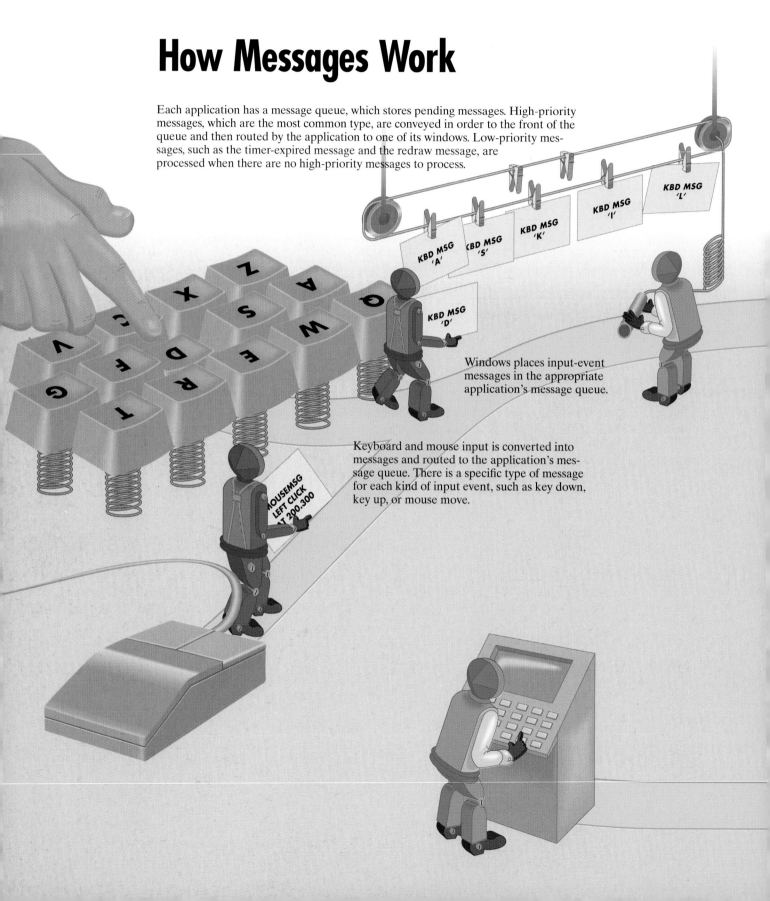

Windows places input-event messages in the appropriate application's message queue.

Keyboard and mouse input is converted into messages and routed to the application's message queue. There is a specific type of message for each kind of input event, such as key down, key up, or mouse move.

Each application is responsible for removing messages from the queue and routing them to the specified window.

Each window is managed by software that knows how to react to messages. For example, this spreadsheet window is about to receive a mouse-left-button-click message. If the click is in one of the spreadsheet cells, then that cell will be selected.

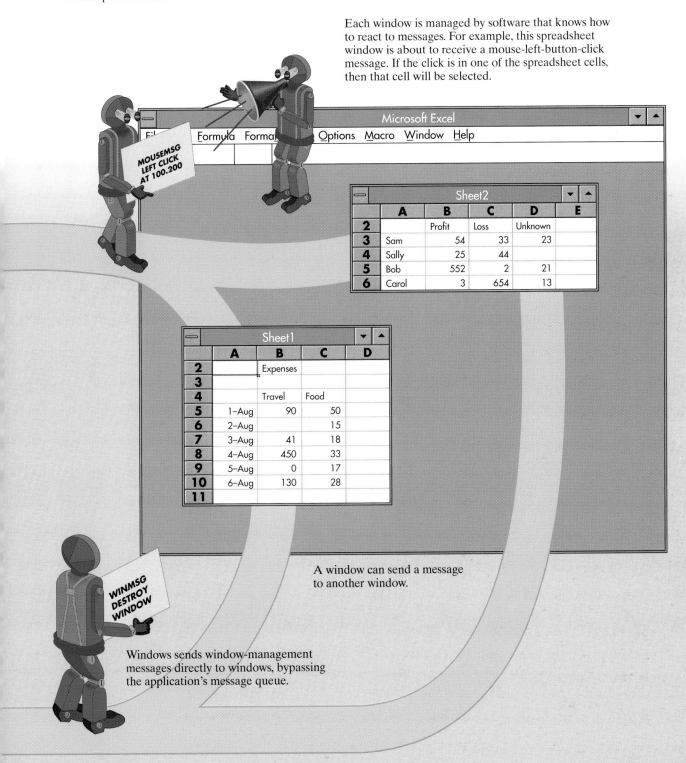

MOUSEMSG LEFT CLICK AT 100.200

A window can send a message to another window.

WINMSG DESTROY WINDOW

Windows sends window-management messages directly to windows, bypassing the application's message queue.

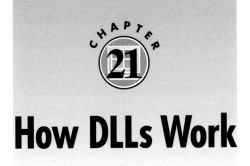

How DLLs Work

WHEN YOU FIRST bought your computer system, you probably had little idea what range of tasks it could perform. But you surely understood the importance of buying an expandable computer. Typical users add fax modems, CD-ROM drives, larger hard disks, more memory, page scanners, printers, graphics tablets, enhanced displays, and the like, to extend the range of their machine. In fact, it's the ease of expansion of the PC architecture that is one of its most impressive features.

Because expansion is so important, the Windows system was written so it could easily be extended. This lets Windows expand to accommodate new features, such as the multimedia features discussed in Part 5 of this book. It also lets software developers add their own features to Windows. For example, all of the programs sold by Lotus use a common spelling checker, which is provided by grafting the Lotus spelling checker onto Windows.

It is surprisingly difficult to make complex software such as Windows expandable. Software is composed of a web of interlocking functions. Each function knows how to perform one well-defined task. To perform a task, one function will often call on the services of another. This is like an office building in which the person in each office performs one specific task, and each person knows where to go to have other tasks performed. But in an office building, it's easy to move the mailroom from one place to another, or to change someone's telephone extension, because people can adapt easily to such simple changes. In most software, all the instructions are coded in at the outset, and changes usually are not permitted.

The key to expansion in Windows is the dynamic link library (DLL). The term DLL is software developer jargon that has escaped to the mainstream. *Dynamic* refers to something that happens when software is being executed; *link* refers to how one software routine finds out the address of another; and a *library* is a collection of software routines. Thus, a *DLL* is a library of software routines that is written specifically to be loaded into Windows while Windows is running, thereby adding some new capability to Windows. DLLs are very similar to .EXE (executable) files that contain Windows applications. The difference is that .EXE files are loaded when you start an application, and they serve your needs; DLLs are loaded when necessary by applications, and they serve applications' needs.

Every DLL contains a table of function names and locations, so that specific functions can easily be located and used. For example, suppose that an application wants to use Lotus's spelling checker DLL to check the spelling of a word. First, the program will tell Windows that it intends to use the Lotus spelling checker DLL. If the DLL is already loaded, then Windows will immediately reply "OK." If it's not already loaded, Windows will load it and then reply "OK." (If it can't be loaded, Windows will reply "Sorry, can't load it.") Once the DLL is in memory, the program asks Windows to use the *check word* function in the spelling checker DLL. Windows will examine the spelling checker DLL's table of functions, find the location of the check word function, and then call that function to check a word's spelling. This sounds like a lot of work, but remember that this process is very similar to how we would find out the new location of the mailroom.

Because DLLs can be loaded and unloaded as necessary, many large programs use them extensively to conserve memory. For example, the Ami Pro word processor contains about 30 DLLs. Only a few of them are loaded at once, greatly reducing Ami Pro's appetite for memory.

DLLs also help developers produce customized versions of a program. For example, all of a program's text messages can be put in a DLL. Then the developer can prepare versions of that DLL in multiple languages, for example, English, French, and German. During program installation, the correct-language DLL is loaded onto the user's computer, automatically creating a version of the program in the user's own language.

Windows itself makes extensive use of DLLs; both USER.EXE and GDI.EXE are DLLs, as are all of Windows's device drivers, such as DISPLAY.DRV and KEYBOARD.DRV. Using DLLs for device drivers helps Windows adapt to the various hardware configurations. For example, there are versions of DISPLAY.DRV for each type of graphics display. During Windows installation (or during system reconfiguration), a specific display driver is renamed DISPLAY.DRV. When Windows next starts, it automatically loads the DISPLAY.DRV dynamic link library, thereby making use of the selected display driver.

How DLLs Work

A dynamic link library (DLL) is software that can be loaded into Windows to provide it with additional features. Once a DLL is loaded, its services are available to all applications, just like Windows's standard services.

DLLs can be loaded into Windows at any time. A few standard DLLs are loaded into Windows when it boots; most DLLs are loaded at the request of a running application program.

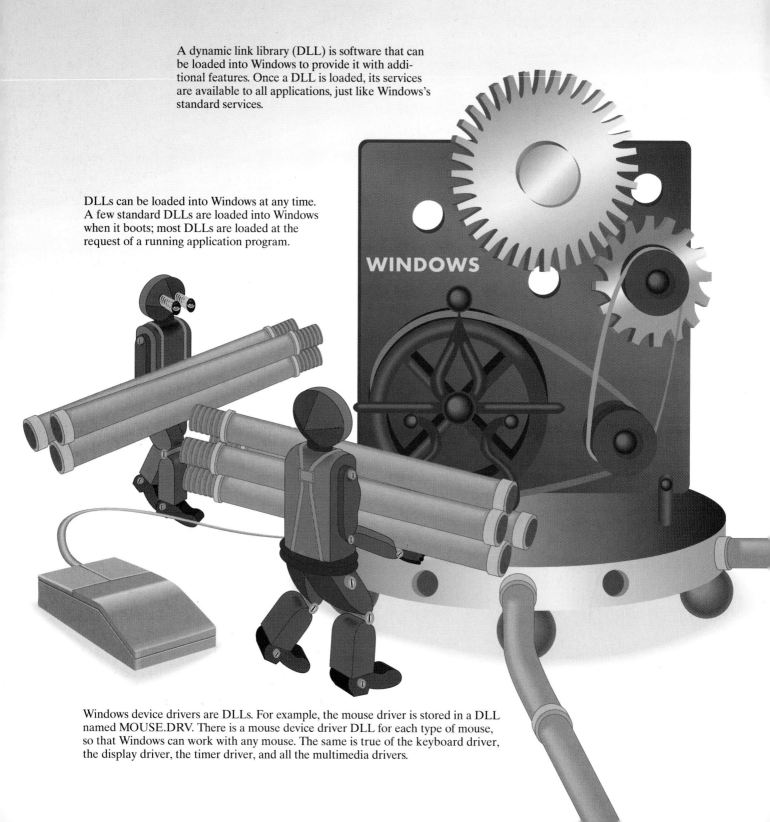

Windows device drivers are DLLs. For example, the mouse driver is stored in a DLL named MOUSE.DRV. There is a mouse device driver DLL for each type of mouse, so that Windows can work with any mouse. The same is true of the keyboard driver, the display driver, the timer driver, and all the multimedia drivers.

SpellCheck DLL

- Init
- Select Dictionary
- Check Word
- Check Document
- Clean Up

A DLL contains a table that lists all of the DLL's accessible functions. When an application uses a function in a DLL, it uses the table to find that function's location.

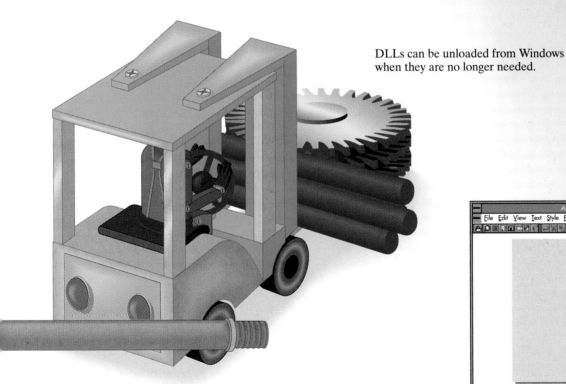

DLLs can be unloaded from Windows when they are no longer needed.

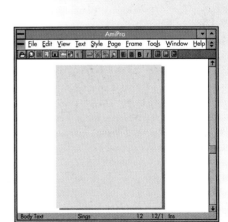

Applications can ask Windows to load DLLs when they are needed. Once a DLL is loaded, an application can access its services. Families of applications often provide common services in DLLs, instead of duplicating those services in each application program. DLLs are also used to customize and internationalize applications. For example, all the language-specific parts of an application can be placed in a DLL, and then versions of that DLL can be prepared in each supported language.

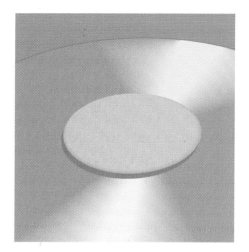

How Virtual Memory Works

WINDOWS CAN DISPLAY and run several programs at the same time, which makes it easy for you to switch from one task to another. Windows uses graphics to make programs easy to use. And, Windows uses typefaces, which make the screen easy to read—and what you see on the screen is exactly what will be printed. These and many other features of Windows are all linked by a common requirement—memory.

To Windows, memory is like floor space in a factory, making it possible for Windows to accommodate new demands. For example, if you start to use a new typeface in a document, Windows is obliged to read the typeface description from disk and ready the individual symbols for use, which requires a significant chunk of the computer's main memory. Similarly, starting a new application requires memory, displaying a dialog box requires memory, and so on. The more you're doing in Windows, the more space it takes.

For Windows to work efficiently, it needs a lot of memory. Most experts suggest that about 2 megabytes of main memory is the minimum amount to run Windows, 4 megabytes is a more reasonable amount, and more than 4, as you'd expect, is even better. Main memory is also called RAM, because it is located in random access memory chips. What's vexing, from Windows's point of view, is that memory demands are so variable. Like demands on the power grid during a heat wave, memory demands on Windows peak when you are doing a lot of things at once. Running five applications takes much more space than running just two; using a dozen typefaces takes more memory than using just a few.

When one region of the country is in a heat wave and running low on power, its power authority often tries to import power from neighboring regions to keep the air conditioners humming. Windows does the same thing; when demand for memory exceeds the memory that's actually installed in the PC, Windows borrows some space from the disk. This technique is called virtual memory, because Windows is able to behave as if it had more memory than the amount of main memory that is installed.

Windows makes use of virtual memory only when it is operating in enhanced mode. To see if your system is in enhanced mode, switch to Program Manager and select About Program Manager from the Help menu. The bottom of the About dialog box shows the current operating mode, and it also shows how much memory is currently free. In enhanced mode, which is the normal mode for most users, the amount of free memory sometimes exceeds the amount of main memory, because Windows sees the total memory pool as the main memory plus the space on disk serving as virtual memory. In standard mode, which is the other mode of operation, Windows doesn't support virtual memory.

You can configure the virtual memory for your PC using the 386 Enhanced applet on the Control Panel. On that applet, press the Virtual Memory button to bring up the Virtual Memory dialog box, which lets you view and change the size of the disk region that's used for virtual memory. You can use a permanent file for virtual memory, which lets Windows boot a little faster, or you can use a temporary file, which is created automatically each time Windows boots.

Windows supports virtual memory by dividing memory into 4,096-byte pages. Each page is either resident in main memory or temporarily copied to disk. If an application tries to use a page that is currently stored on disk, Windows will automatically copy the page back to main memory, making it available. To make room in main memory for a new page, Windows usually must copy some other page to disk.

Virtual memory works best when almost all of the active pages fit into main memory—in other words, when the pages stored on disk are mostly inactive. Virtual memory doesn't work well when pages are incessantly copied back and forth, which is called thrashing. Because copying a page from disk to main memory is about a thousand times slower than accessing a page already in main memory, thrashing can slow your PC to less than a crawl.

How Virtual Memory Works

Memory is divided into 4,096-byte pages. Pages are either resident in main memory, which means they are instantly accessible, or they are temporarily stored on disk. If stored on disk, they can't be used by a program or by Windows until they are copied back to main memory, which takes 10 or 20 milliseconds.

Virtual memory allows Windows to behave as if it had more memory than is actually installed in your PC. This is accomplished by using disk storage as an extension of main memory. However, the disk can only store information that is not currently in use.

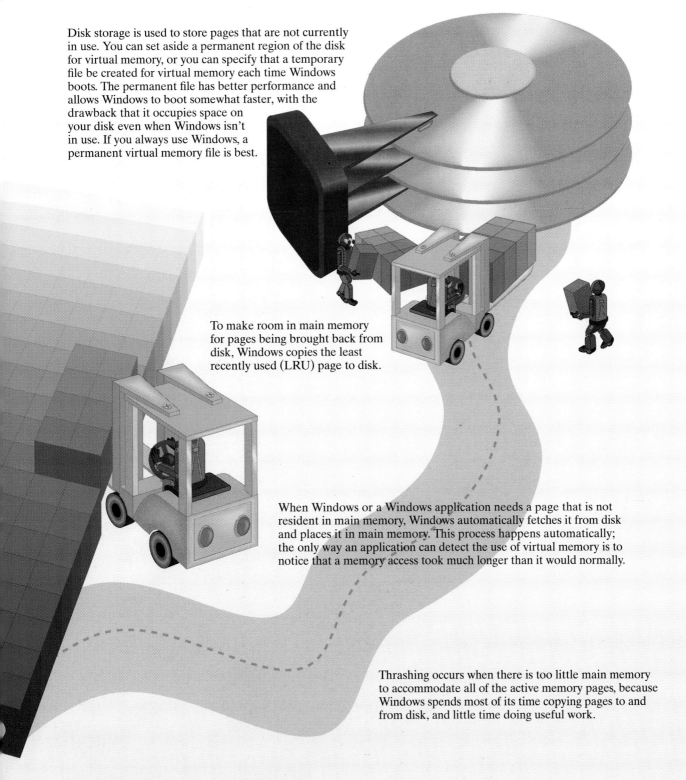

Disk storage is used to store pages that are not currently in use. You can set aside a permanent region of the disk for virtual memory, or you can specify that a temporary file be created for virtual memory each time Windows boots. The permanent file has better performance and allows Windows to boot somewhat faster, with the drawback that it occupies space on your disk even when Windows isn't in use. If you always use Windows, a permanent virtual memory file is best.

To make room in main memory for pages being brought back from disk, Windows copies the least recently used (LRU) page to disk.

When Windows or a Windows application needs a page that is not resident in main memory, Windows automatically fetches it from disk and places it in main memory. This process happens automatically; the only way an application can detect the use of virtual memory is to notice that a memory access took much longer than it would normally.

Thrashing occurs when there is too little main memory to accommodate all of the active memory pages, because Windows spends most of its time copying pages to and from disk, and little time doing useful work.

Windows manages virtual memory automatically. You can specify the size and type of the virtual memory file by using the Control Panel's 386 Enhanced applet.

How Input and Output Device Drivers Work

NPUT AND OUTPUT (I/O) are vital, though not very glamorous, operations in any computer system. In Windows, the I/O devices can be divided into two camps: one for storage devices (disks, tapes, CD-ROMs) and one for user interface devices, such as the screen, keyboard, mouse, sound board, and so on.

Storage-device I/O in Windows is organized much like that in any other computer system. For each type of storage device, there is a device driver software module. The device driver knows all the details of sending information to and reading information from the device. Whenever an I/O operation to a disk or tape is needed, Windows passes the request to the device driver, the device driver accesses the device hardware, and then the operation is performed.

User-interface I/O operations in Windows are much more interesting than storage-device I/O, because they are an integral part of the most interesting part of Windows, the graphical user interface. Output to the display has already been covered (Chapter 4), as has input and output to multimedia devices (Part 5). Thus, in this chapter, the focus will be on some remaining devices: the mouse, keyboard, and printer.

The mouse is the simplest of these three. The mouse driver software is a dynamic link library (DLL) that is loaded while Windows is booting. There is a different mouse driver DLL for each type of mouse. The appropriate mouse driver for your mouse was copied into the Windows System directory when Windows was first installed. During the bootstrap process, Windows loads the mouse driver and makes sure that it is able to sense the mouse. If the mouse is not connected or not functioning properly, you'll be notified as Windows boots.

As you move the mouse across your desk, the hardware circuitry in the mouse codes the motion in a series of digital pulses that travel down the mouse cable (the tail!) to the computer. In the computer, the mouse driver software decodes these pulses to reconstruct the mouse's motion and the button presses. Next, the mouse driver software calls Windows and reports the changes. Windows, not the driver, then sends a mouse click or mouse move message to the topmost application window at the mouse's position.

The keyboard is managed similarly to the mouse. For each type of keyboard, there is a specific DLL software driver that is loaded when Windows boots. The keyboard driver performs a few simple tests to make sure that the keyboard is working, and then it loads language-specific and keyboard-specific translation tables. The keyboard-specific translation table accounts for slightly different layouts of otherwise similar keyboards, and the language-specific translation table produces the appropriate accented characters for each language.

Every PC keyboard contains a tiny special-purpose microprocessor that sends key up and key down information to the PC. In the PC, the keyboard driver decodes the information to determine what keys have been pressed. At this stage, the key press information is in a very crude form, which is called the scan code. Knowing the scan code is equivalent to knowing that the third key from the left in the second row was pressed. Next, the keyboard driver uses the two translation tables to translate the scan code into the Windows key code. This sounds like a lot of extra work, but it's this generality that makes it easy, using the Control Panel's International applet, to switch from one language's symbols and native keyboard layout to another.

Again parallel to the mouse, the keyboard driver simply notifies Windows when there are key presses and key releases and leaves to Windows the task of composing keyboard messages and sending them to the appropriate application. Thus, the keyboard driver plays a central role in adapting Windows to work in other languages, although it is not intimately involved in the messaging aspects of the user interface.

The printer driver is one of the most complex areas in Windows. Like other drivers, the printer driver is a DLL. But it is much more complex than the mouse or keyboard driver, because it must adapt all of the graphics facilities in Windows to a specific printer. The printer driver, like the display driver, must be able to carry out every graphics operation provided by Windows. The only difference is that the display driver performs the graphics operations on the display screen, and the printer driver does so for a specific printer.

The printer driver is unlike other drivers in several ways. First, it is not responsible for providing a hardware interface to the printer. Instead, the printer driver typically sends its output to a print spooler, usually the Windows print spooler. The print spooler temporarily stores each print job on disk, sending each in turn to the printer.

Second, there are many printers and printerlike devices, such as fax machines, that are often attached and in use at once. Thus Windows doesn't load a single printer driver when it boots, but rather it loads and unloads them as applications issue print requests, and it often loads more than one at a time. That's why you can select specific printers from within an application, usually using the Printer Setup dialog box, which you often access from the application's File menu.

How the Mouse and Keyboard Drivers Work

The output of the mouse is an electrical signal that is sent to a standard PC serial port (for serial mice) or to a special mouse interface circuit in the PC.

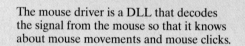

The mouse driver is a DLL that decodes the signal from the mouse so that it knows about mouse movements and mouse clicks.

In most mice, there is a hard rubber ball that spins as you move the mouse. A sensor in the mouse senses the movement, and electronics in the mouse create an electrical signal that represents the movement.

When the mouse position changes, or when the mouse's buttons are pressed or released, the mouse driver notifies the Windows kernel of the changes. It is up to the kernel to send mouse movement or mouse button press messages to the topmost window under the mouse.

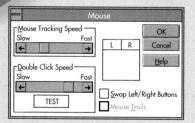

The Control Panel's Mouse applet lets you control the mouse sensitivity. It communicates with the driver to inform it of new settings so they take effect immediately. The Mouse applet stores mouse configuration settings in the WIN.INI configuration file.

PC keyboards contain a microprocessor that continually scans all of the keys. When a key is pressed or released, the microprocessor sends an electrical signal to the host PC. The keyboard's microprocessor also receives signals from the PC that tell it to turn the keyboard status lights on and off.

The Control Panel's Keyboard applet lets you control key repeat.

The keyboard driver is a DLL. Its first task is to decode the scan code signal from the keyboard.

The keyboard driver's second task is to translate the scan code into a key code, using a keyboard-specific translation table and a language-specific translation table, both of which are contained in DLLs.

The Control Panel's International applet lets you specify your keyboard's layout and the language that you want to use. This information is passed to the keyboard driver so it can use the indicated translation DLLs.

After key presses and releases are translated, the resulting key codes are passed to Windows. It is Windows's job to create keyboard messages and send these messages to the appropriate window.

How Printer Drivers Work

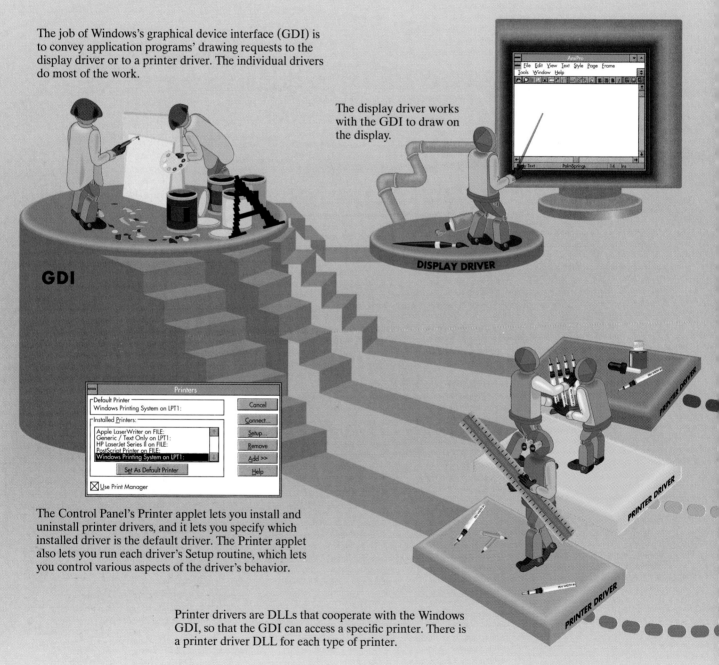

The job of Windows's graphical device interface (GDI) is to convey application programs' drawing requests to the display driver or to a printer driver. The individual drivers do most of the work.

The display driver works with the GDI to draw on the display.

DISPLAY DRIVER

GDI

Printers

Default Printer
Windows Printing System on LPT1:

Installed Printers:

Apple LaserWriter on FILE:
Generic / Text Only on LPT1:
HP LaserJet Series II on FILE:
PostScript Printer on FILE:
Windows Printing System on LPT1:

Set As Default Printer

☒ Use Print Manager

Cancel
Connect...
Setup...
Remove
Add >>
Help

PRINTER DRIVER

PRINTER DRIVER

PRINTER DRIVER

The Control Panel's Printer applet lets you install and uninstall printer drivers, and it lets you specify which installed driver is the default driver. The Printer applet also lets you run each driver's Setup routine, which lets you control various aspects of the driver's behavior.

Printer drivers are DLLs that cooperate with the Windows GDI, so that the GDI can access a specific printer. There is a printer driver DLL for each type of printer.

Printer drivers are loaded and unloaded dynamically, depending on the application's print requests.

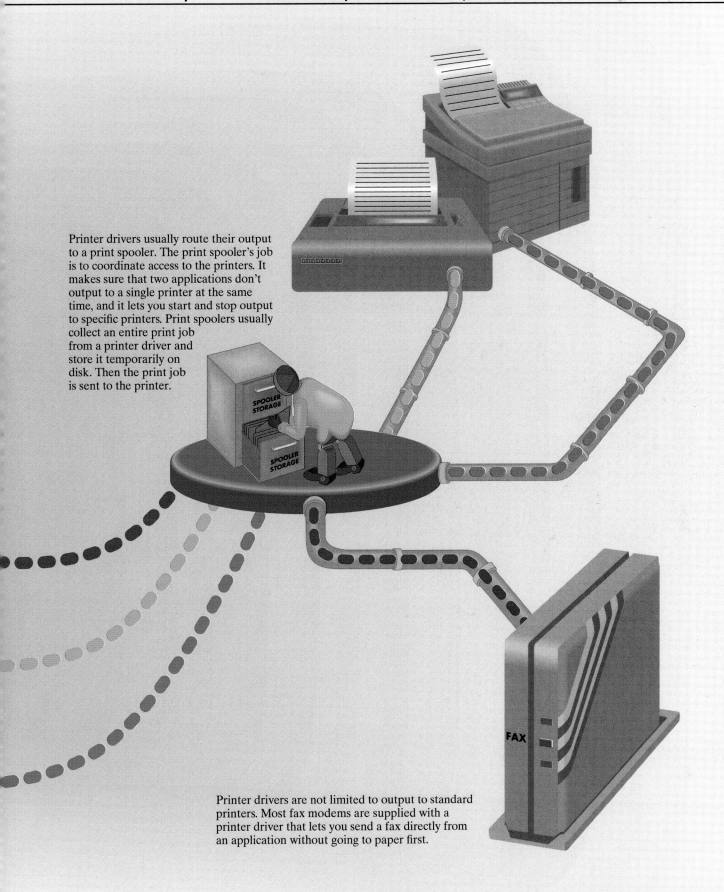

Printer drivers usually route their output to a print spooler. The print spooler's job is to coordinate access to the printers. It makes sure that two applications don't output to a single printer at the same time, and it lets you start and stop output to specific printers. Print spoolers usually collect an entire print job from a printer driver and store it temporarily on disk. Then the print job is sent to the printer.

SPOOLER STORAGE

SPOOLER STORAGE

FAX

Printer drivers are not limited to output to standard printers. Most fax modems are supplied with a printer driver that lets you send a fax directly from an application without going to paper first.

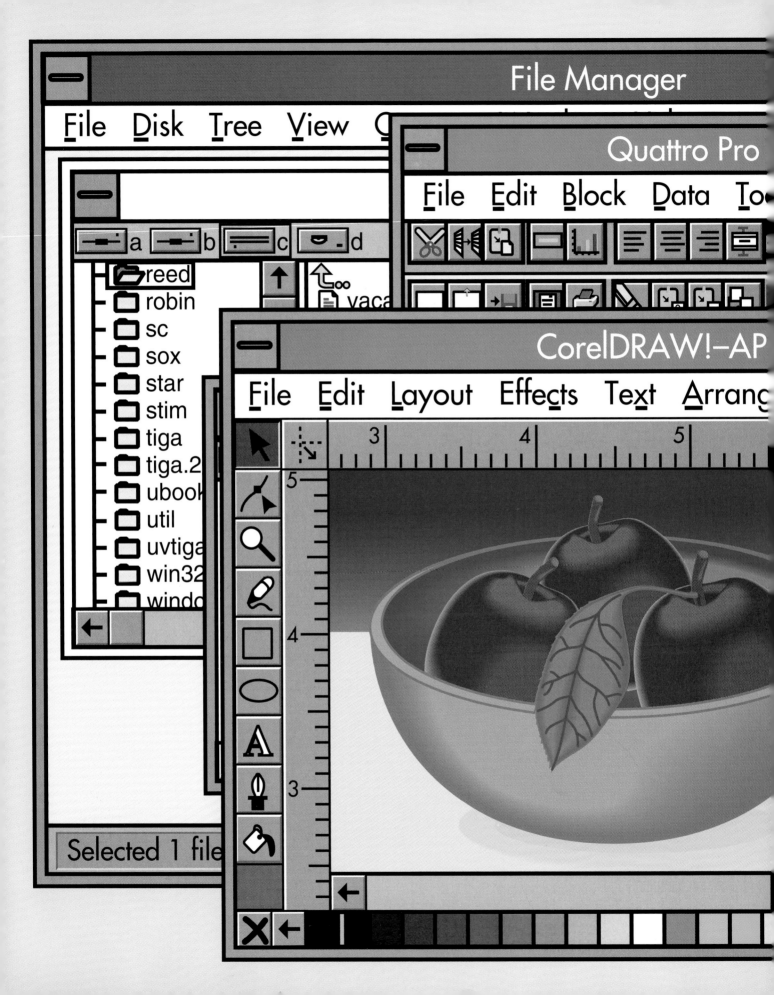

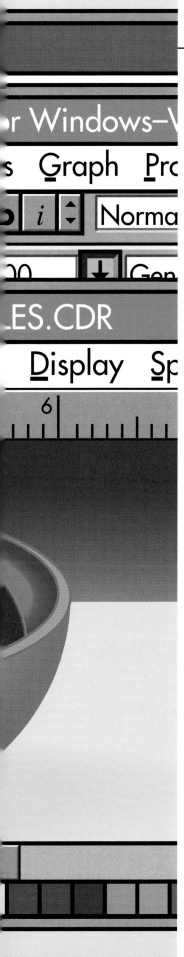

RUNNING APPLICATIONS

7

CONTENTS

Chapter 24: How Windows Runs Windows Applications
176

Chapter 25: How Windows Runs DOS Applications
182

Chapter 26: How Multitasking Works
188

OVERVIEW

WINDOWS HAS MANY roles that contribute to its primary role, running applications. All the facets of Windows that we've covered earlier in the book—graphics, typography, multimedia, the user interface, messaging, and so on—help create an environment in which application programs can thrive.

From Windows's vantage point, there are two very different types of applications that it must serve: true Windows applications and DOS applications. Windows applications are true graphical applications; written specifically for Windows, they directly access Windows services. DOS applications are programs that were originally written for the older DOS operating system. They don't take advantage of Windows directly, but many still serve vital functions that aren't yet duplicated by Windows programs.

Because Windows applications and DOS applications operate very differently, Windows must manage them individually. For true Windows applications, Windows must provide a whole gamut of services, from helping with menus to playing multimedia audio and video clips. For DOS applications, Windows must mimic, to a painstaking level of detail, the environment provided by DOS. Because these two approaches are so different, each is covered in a separate chapter.

Windows doesn't merely provide an environment in which a single application program can operate, but rather, it lets several application programs operate at the same time. This is a key to boosting your productivity, because it lets you use several programs in combination as necessary for your work. Running several applications at once also lets you keep a calendar, a phone log, and an appointment book ready and waiting, because in today's world we are often interrupted and often distracted and need to work on several things at once.

How Windows Runs Windows Applications

WHEN WINDOWS RUNS an application specifically written for the Windows environment, its first step is to locate the application's executable (.EXE) file. The .EXE file usually contains the instructions that create the application's main window and performs other chores that help the application start operating. Windows sets aside enough space in memory for all the instructions in the application's .EXE file, and then it loads these instructions into memory.

Once the main part of an application is loaded into memory, Windows makes the application start to execute. This is the step where the application springs to life. Your computer's processor chip starts to follow the instructions built into the application. Usually, the application repeatedly asks Windows to do tasks, such as draw menus or create windows; the application and Windows alternate, engaging in a give-and-take relationship.

When it first starts to execute, each application has many chores to perform in order to be ready for you to start using it. For example, during initialization, a typical application will create windows, menus, scroll bars, and other user interface components. It will probably retrieve configuration settings from .INI files, load any necessary .DLL files, and so on. During this early phase of operation, which usually lasts only a second or two, the application is clearly in charge, and Windows is doing the application's bidding.

Once an application is fully formed and ready for you to use it, the relationships reverse. During the second, much longer phase, most applications spend their time waiting for input messages. When input events occur, the application responds as necessary and then resumes its wait for further input. During this second phase, Windows is clearly in charge, because it manages and routes all the mouse and keyboard traffic. Thus, for most of their life, applications take on a more passive role.

As you will see in Chapter 26, having applications wait for input events is a key aspect of how Windows runs several Windows applications at a time. When an application is waiting for an input event, it's idle, which gives other applications (or Windows itself) a chance to operate. Some programs need to operate continuously, even when they aren't receiving input. For example, a program showing animation needs to constantly update the display. In Windows, this is best accomplished using a timer. When a timer expires, the application gets a time-out message. In response, it does some work, and then it schedules itself for another timer message.

Windows executable files are an important asset to executing Windows applications. A .EXE file doesn't only contain instructions; it also is likely to contain many Windows resources, such as menus, icons, and dialog boxes, which are used while the application is executing. For example, an application's main menu is usually stored in its .EXE file. Each .EXE file is organized like a reference book with a good index so that it is easy to locate the resources it contains. Whenever the application needs to use a resource from the .EXE file, Windows will consult the .EXE's index, turn to the right "page," and retrieve the specified resource.

It's possible for a software company to deliver a useful Windows application that consists of a single .EXE file, but it isn't very practical. Instead, most applications are split into many pieces so that they are more manageable. For example, a software developer might put all of a program's text messages into a separate file. This would allow the vendor to internationalize the application by changing just that one file, leaving all other files untouched.

Programs are also partitioned into may files because of the *90/10 rule*. This maxim suggests that 10 percent of the program's features are used 90 percent of the time, and the other 90 percent of the features are used just 10 percent of the time. Thus, most software vendors put the instructions for all the seldom-used features into separate dynamic link library (.DLL) files (discussed in Chapter 21). For example, Borland's Quattro Pro spreadsheet is shipped with about 30 .DLL files that supplement the instructions in the application's main .EXE file. While Quattro Pro is executing, Windows loads and then unloads the .DLL files as necessary.

How Windows Runs Windows Applications

.DLL files let an application load and unload its parts as necessary. They also help with problems such as customization and internationalization, because it is easy to replace individual .DLLs to meet specific needs.

Most applications use dynamic link library (.DLL) files to provide some of their features. A .DLL file has the same structure as an .EXE file.

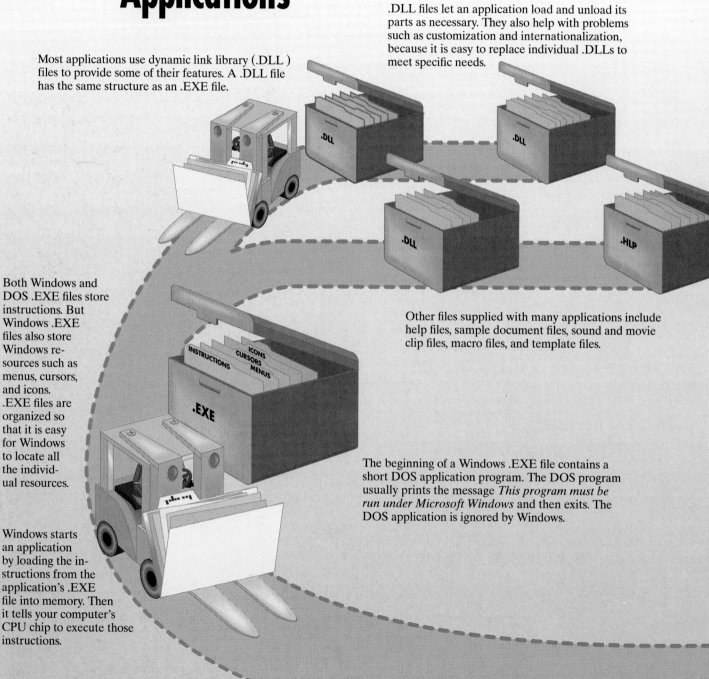

Both Windows and DOS .EXE files store instructions. But Windows .EXE files also store Windows resources such as menus, cursors, and icons. .EXE files are organized so that it is easy for Windows to locate all the individual resources.

Other files supplied with many applications include help files, sample document files, sound and movie clip files, macro files, and template files.

The beginning of a Windows .EXE file contains a short DOS application program. The DOS program usually prints the message *This program must be run under Microsoft Windows* and then exits. The DOS application is ignored by Windows.

Windows starts an application by loading the instructions from the application's .EXE file into memory. Then it tells your computer's CPU chip to execute those instructions.

Chapter 24: How Windows Runs Windows Applications 181

Once an application has finished initializing, it enters a more reactive state in which it waits for messages to arrive. Each time a message arrives, the application processes the message and then waits for another message to arrive. Waiting for messages is important because it gives other Windows applications a chance to execute, which is how Windows runs several applications at once.

When an application first starts to execute, it busily works with Windows to create its main window, to load menus and other resources, and to perform other initialization chores. During this phase of operation, which typically lasts only a few seconds or less, the application follows its own plan of operation.

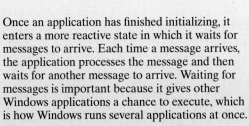

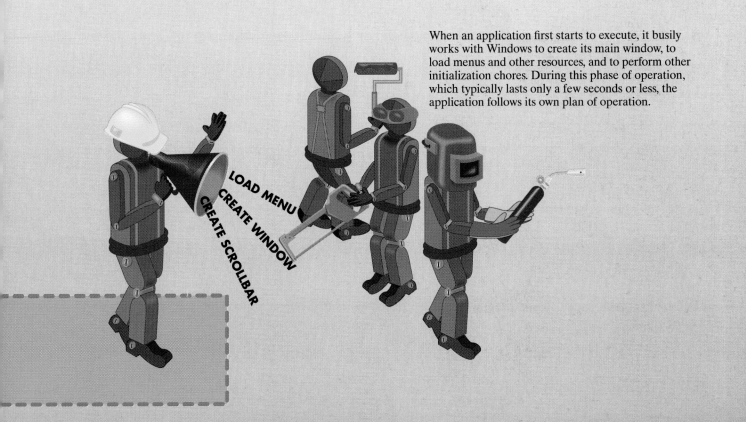

LOAD MENU
CREATE WINDOW
CREATE SCROLLBAR

CHAPTER
25

How Windows Runs DOS Applications

DURING THE MID to late eighties, tens of thousands of DOS software applications were developed and widely deployed. This software bounty helped create the market for desktop computer systems. Preserving the huge value of the existing DOS software base was an important consideration for the Windows design team. Therefore, they made it possible for Windows to run DOS applications.

Running a DOS application within Windows is very different from running a Windows application in Windows. When Windows runs a native Windows application, standard Windows components (the application .EXE file and its resources such as menus, fonts, and dialogs; its DLLs; its help files; and so forth) are orchestrated by Windows to provide you with a graphical environment. This is a complex endeavor, but it's not all that remarkable that software components, specially built for the purpose, work smoothly together.

When Windows runs a DOS application, however, it can't dictate to the application how it should operate. Instead, all DOS applications follow a melody that was written by IBM in the early eighties, when they first designed the IBM PC. Since then, DOS applications have followed that original score with remarkably few chord changes. Thus, the role that Windows must play is that of mimic—it must construct, within the Windows environment, a perfect imitation of IBM's original PC.

Fortunately, long before Windows was conceived, Intel realized that each time it released a newer, faster, better CPU chip, it had to build in compatibility with its previous models. Thus, there are hardware facilities in all the newer Intel CPU chips that help Windows to recreate, in painstaking detail, the original PC.

In PCs based on the Intel 386 or later, the CPU has an operating mode called virtual-86 mode. When the CPU is in virtual-86 mode, it behaves nearly identically to the 8088 chip used in the original IBM PC. (The mode is called virtual-86 because it imitates the 8086 family of CPUs, of which the 8088 is the most popular member.) Thus, Intel's virtual-86 mode provides one aspect of the solution; it mimics the operation of the original CPU.

But there's more to the problem than just mimicking the CPU; Windows also has to mimic all the hardware devices that are commonly used by DOS programs. Windows meets this need primarily by supplying virtual device drivers, which are called VxDs. (The *V* is for *virtual*; the *D* is for *Device* or *Driver*, take your pick; and in a specific VxD, the *x* is replaced by the name of a device.) The name notwithstanding, most VxDs used to run DOS applications are not true device drivers, but more often, they are arbitrators and facilitators, providing access to a device in an orderly manner for multiple DOS sessions. This all makes sense when you remember that DOS and DOS applications already provide their own drivers for all these devices.

From the point of view of emulating the original PC, the most problematic device is the display. To facilitate screen output from DOS applications, Windows uses two helper programs. The names vary slightly, but these two helper programs are named similarly to WINOA386.MOD and VGA.3GR. (The names are coded: *WINOA* stands for *windows old application* and the 386 signifies use in Windows enhanced mode, which is only available on the 386 or later CPU; *VGA* signifies the VGA display adapter, and *3GR* signifies a screen grabber for Windows enhanced mode.) WINOA386 works together with the screen grabber to make the DOS application's screen output appear on your Windows screen, and to provide other standard services such as cut and paste and the print screen function.

When you run a DOS application from within Windows, Windows ties all these pieces together. It creates a virtual-86 environment that is connected to VxDs, connected to winoa386, connected to the DOS system software, and so forth. Such an environment is called a virtual machine, and Windows creates one for each DOS command line session, or DOS application, that you run.

Virtual machines don't all behave identically. For example, some virtual machines provide extra memory for DOS applications that are memory gluttons. This feature of Windows is controlled using program information files (PIFs). If you run a DOS application that doesn't have a .PIF, then the virtual machine will be configured according to _DEFAULT.PIF, which is stored in the Windows directory. If a DOS application has special needs for memory usage or the like, then it must have a .PIF. You can edit or create .PIFs using the Windows PIF Editor.

Within an 8086 virtual machine, none of the usual Windows techniques are used. Virtual machines don't use messaging; they don't use menus or other resources; and they don't have access to Windows's graphical features. Windows even uses a different form of multitasking for DOS sessions. Instead of Windows's usual cooperative multitasking, which is the norm for native Windows applications, virtual 8086 machines are subject to preemptive multitasking. (Multitasking will discussed in the next chapter.)

How Windows Runs DOS Applications

Windows runs DOS applications by crafting an environment that mimics that of the original IBM PC. This environment, known as a virtual machine, lets a DOS application run as if it were running in DOS. Windows accomplishes this mimicry using advanced hardware features from modern computer CPUs, plus specially written software drivers and helper programs.

The System Menu control on a DOS application's window lets you perform cut and paste operations, it lets you specify the size of the typeface that is used in the DOS window, and it gives you limited control over other aspects of how the DOS application runs. For more control, you must edit (or create) the DOS application's .PIF.

When the DOS application is displayed in a window, the window frame and title bar are drawn by Windows. The frame and title bar are absent when the application is displayed full screen.

You can press Alt+Enter to switch a DOS application between full screen and a window.

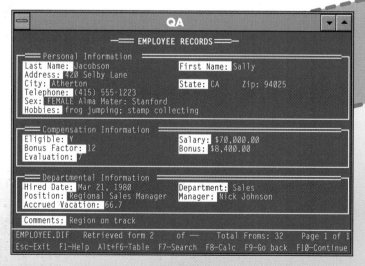

The interior of a DOS window is controlled by the DOS application. Symantec's Q&A application (a combination database and word processor) is running in this DOS window. When you switch to this DOS window, all of Q&A's menu and keyboard commands become active, just as if you were using Q&A under DOS.

Windows uses software modules called virtual device drivers (VxDs) to mediate access to hardware devices. Some VxDs imitate hardware features found in the IBM PC, whereas others are more like arbitrators that allow multiple DOS sessions to access a single device.

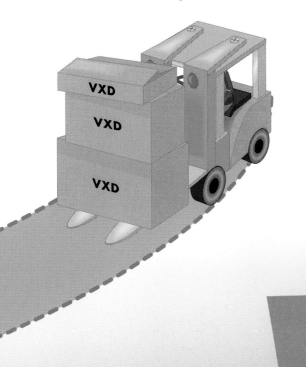

Windows uses program information files (PIFs) to specify the characteristics of virtual machines. For example, PIFs specify whether an application starts full screen or in a window, how much memory is required, and so forth. DOS applications that don't have their own PIF are executed using the settings in _DEFAULT.PIF. You can use the Windows PIF Editor to change settings in an application's PIF.

Just before Windows switches to a DOS application running within a virtual machine, it tells the CPU to switch to virtual-86 mode of operation. In virtual-86 mode, the CPU executes instructions and otherwise behaves almost identically to the 8088 processor found in the original IBM PC. This step is necessary because DOS applications contain instructions that operate differently in Windows, which usually uses the CPU's enhanced mode of operation, than they do in virtual-86 mode.

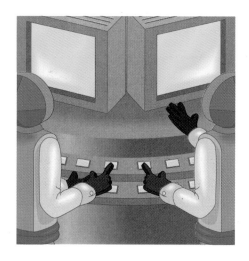

CHAPTER 26

How Multitasking Works

ONE OF WINDOWS'S most useful features, and also one of its most natural and comfortable features, is multitasking. In a multitasking computer system, the computer is able to run more than one program at a time. For example, in Windows you might have an appointment calendar, a word processor, a spreadsheet, a mail program, and a communications program all active at once. You can start a file transfer using the communications program, or you can issue a complex data retrieval request using the database, and then switch to another application while those programs carry out their chores.

Multitasking is natural in a computer system, because it's what you do all day long even off the computer. Of course, there are occasional times when you concentrate on one task for an extended period, but for most office staff and other people who work with computers, interruptions are the rule, not the exception. For example, if your supervisor calls to schedule a meeting while you're juggling expenses using your spreadsheet, you can instantly switch to your calendar program to set up an appointment.

In a computer with several processors, it's possible to run different tasks on each processor, so that each task is truly running at the same time. Multiple-processor computers are becoming widely used as file servers and as other shared resources, but today they are seldom used as personal desktop machines.

In a computer with only a single CPU, multitasking must be accomplished by switching rapidly from one task to another. If the switching occurs rapidly enough, usually many times each second, it gives the impression that the programs are running simultaneously.

Computer systems implement multitasking using two basic approaches. The first approach, called cooperative multitasking, lets the applications decide when to relinquish control of the CPU so that another application can do some work. In a cooperative multitasking system, which is how Windows multitasks native Windows applications, the currently executing task continues to execute until it decides to relinquish control.

The drawback of cooperative multitasking is that a single program can hog the system by refusing to relinquish control to other tasks. Ironically, hogging the system can also be seen as an advantage. For example, hogging is desirable when the active program is doing something important that you want done as soon as possible.

Windows must use a different approach, called preemptive multitasking, for multitasking virtual machines that are running DOS applications (see Chapter 25). Remember that one requirement for running DOS applications in Windows is that they must be run as is; modifications are not allowed. Thus, cooperative multitasking of DOS applications is impossible, because DOS applications weren't originally written to relinquish control to other programs.

In preemptive multitasking, Windows uses hardware features of the CPU to implement multitasking. Before switching to a DOS session, Windows tells your computer's timer just how long the DOS session will be allowed to run. When the preset time elapses, Windows automatically regains control and temporarily suspends the DOS session. At this point, Windows is free to do something else, such as run a Windows application. Then a short time later, usually much less than a second, Windows will give the DOS session another slice of time, and then another, and so on. This process is called time slicing, because it's as if each second of time were divided into slices, and each task got some number of time slices each second.

Windows 3.1 uses two approaches to multitasking because it originally had to run on computers that were more limited than most used in business today. Future versions of Windows will make increasing use of preemptive multitasking because it gives users more control over their applications, ultimately letting them get more done.

How Multitasking Works

Windows Switches between Windows Applications Using Cooperative Multitasking

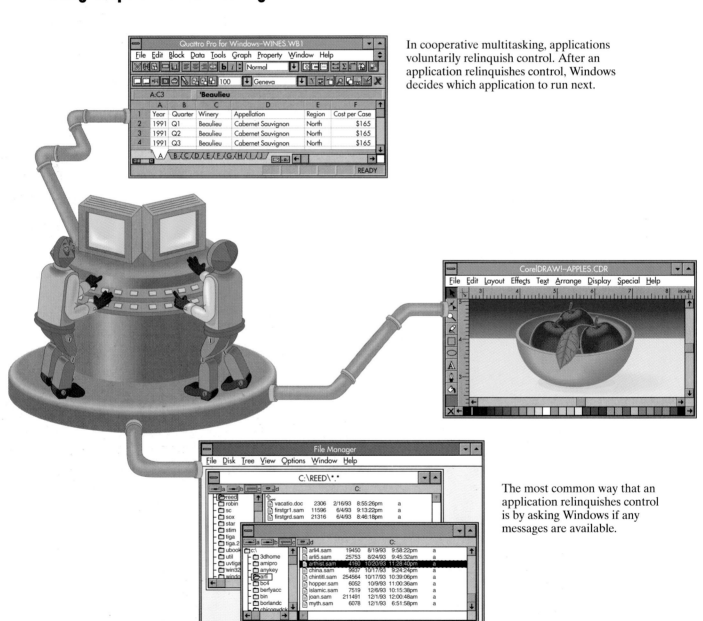

In cooperative multitasking, applications voluntarily relinquish control. After an application relinquishes control, Windows decides which application to run next.

The most common way that an application relinquishes control is by asking Windows if any messages are available.

Windows Switches between DOS Sessions Using Preemptive Multitasking

In preemptive multitasking, control is passed from one program to another automatically. This is accomplished using a timer to measure elapsed time, together with hardware features of the CPU that allow one program to be suspended while another is activated. Windows uses preemptive multitasking to multitask DOS sessions because DOS programs, unlike Windows programs, weren't written to relinquish control.

The timer that Windows uses is a silicon chip in the PC. When the preset time expires, the timer interrupts whatever program is running and automatically switches to the Windows scheduler.

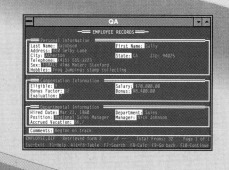

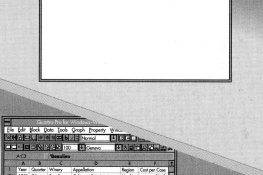

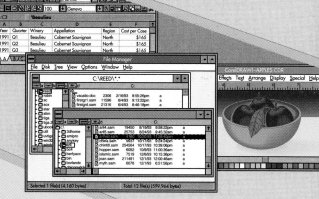

The collection of all the running Windows programs are treated as a single task by the Windows preemptive scheduler. When the collection of Windows programs receives a time slice, the applications multitask cooperatively during that time slice.

A

Accessories group, 75

aliasing, 54

AND bitmaps, 55, 65, 68–69

animation, 137–141

animation cells, 137

animation playback drivers, 138, 141

ANN files, 94

Annotation feature (WinHelp), 94, 97

ANSI character set, 57–58, 60

applets (Control Panel). *See* Control Panel

application groups, 75

application icons, 66, 78–79

application message queue, 147–148, 150–151

applications
  reduced to icons, 30–31, 69
  running, 173–193
  running multiple, 7, 175
  starting, 19, 79, 82, 85
  use of windows, 25–27
  using together with others, 99–119
  vs. utilities, 73

arcs, drawing, 54

arrow pointer, 66

ASCII character set, 57

audio, 123, 125–129

audio board, 126, 128–129

audio clips, 123

audio video interleave (.AVI) files, 132, 135

authoring software, 137, 140

AUTOEXEC.BAT, 15

B

Bartlett's Quotations, 100

BIOS (basic input/output system), 6, 15, 18

bitblits, 50

bit block transfers, 50, 55

BITBLTs, 55

bitmap graphics, 50

bitmaps, 39, 49, 55, 65

blits, 50

BN_CLICKED message, 47

Bookshelf, 100

booting, 15–16, 18–19

brushes, 49, 52

brush styles, 52

built-in Windows utilities, 71–97

button controls, 43

button-press events, 38

bytes, 9

C

capture board (video image), 132, 134

CD-ROM, 123

CD-ROM audio, 126, 128

cells, animation, 137

central processing units. *See* CPUs

character sets, 57–58, 60

circles, drawing, 54

client area, 26, 30

clients
DDE, 109–110
OLE, 116–117, 119

Clipboard, 103–104, 106–107, 118

Clipboard Viewer utility (CLIPBRD.EXE), 103–104, 107

codec (COmpression/DECompression) systems, 131–132

cold DDE pipelines, 109

compound documents, 115, 119

compression, video file, 131–132

CONFIG.SYS, 15

CONTROL.EXE, 90

CONTROL.INI, 90

Control Panel, 73, 87–88, 90–91
International applet, 166, 169
Keyboard applet, 169
Mouse applet, 168
Printer applet, 170
386 Enhanced applet, 160, 163

Control Panel window, 91

controls
button, 43
custom, 43, 46
sending and receiving messages, 44

cooperative multitasking, 189, 192

copying files to disk, 82

copying files between disks, 84

copy and paste, 106

COPYPEN drawing mode, 53

CorelDRAW Photo-Paint, 26, 28–31

CPL files, 87, 90

CPL.INI, 87

CPUs (central processing units), 9–10, 12–13

cursor resources, 65

cursors, 65–66, 68

custom controls, 43, 46

cut and paste, 100, 103–104, 106–107

D

Date & Time dialog box, 91

DDE (dynamic data exchange), 100, 109–110, 112–113
clients, 109–110
network, 110
pipelines, 109
servers, 109–110

decompression, video file, 131–132

Desktop icons, 76, 78

desktop manager, 16, 19

desktop window, 25, 28, 30

device drivers, 15–16, 18–19, 156, 165
animation playback, 138, 141
display, 16, 18, 170
EMS, 13
input, 165
keyboard, 166, 169
mouse, 156, 165, 168
output, 165

printer, 166, 170–171

virtual (VxDs), 184, 187

DialogBox(), 47

dialog box editor, 43

dialog boxes, 43–44

designing, 46

executing, 47

types of, 43

dialog resources, 43, 46

digital video, 131

digitization, 132

digitizer, 125

directories, moving files between, 82

disk icons (File Manager), 84

disks, 82, 84

disk storage, 163

display, Windows, 25–31

display drivers, 16, 18, 170

DISPLAY.DRV, 154

dithering, 49

DLLs (dynamic link libraries), 145, 153–157, 178, 180

document icons, 66, 69

DOS

and Windows, 1–19

memory use, 9–10, 12–13

organization of, 5–7

DOS applications

full-screen or window, 186

running, 175, 183–184, 186–187

drawing, 49–50, 52–55

drawing modes, 53

drivers (device). *See* device drivers

dynamic data exchange. *See* DDE

dynamic link libraries. *See* DLLs

E

Edit windows, 30–31

8088 CPU, 9

80286 and higher CPUs, 9–10, 12–13, 18–19

ellipses, drawing, 54

EMS (expanded memory) drivers, 13

Enhanced mode, 159–160

environment (Windows)

event-driven, 22

provisions of, 73

windows-based, 25–27, 44

event messages. *See* messages

events, 22

EXE files, 79, 153, 177–178, 180

F

fax modems, 171

file compression, video, 131–132

file formats, 104

File Manager, 73, 81–82, 84–85

automatic startup, 81

disk icons, 84

selecting multiple files, 84

status line, 84

files, 81

    copying between disks, 82, 84

    copying to floppy disks, 82

    moving between directories, 82

floppy disks, 82, 84

fonts, 57–63

FOT files, 62

486 CPU

    architecture, 9, 12

    booting, 18–19

G

GDI.EXE, 154

graphical device interface (GDI), 170

graphical interface, 21–69

graphics file formats, 104

grouping applications, 75

group windows, 75, 78

GRP files, 75–76, 78

H

help, accessing, 93, 96

help files, 93–94, 96

Help (Windows), 73, 93–94, 96–97

high-priority messages, 148, 150

hints (for outline typefaces), 59, 63

HLP files, 93–94, 96

hot DDE pipelines, 109

hourglass cursor, 66

I

I-beam cursor, 66

icon resources, 65

icons

    application, 30–31, 66, 69, 78–79

    bitmaps for, 65, 69

    Desktop vs. Program Manager, 76

    reducing documents to, 69

    types of, 66

image-capture board, 132, 134

image resources, 39

INI files, 87, 91

initialization, Windows, 15–16

input device drivers, 165

input device management, 145

input events, 150, 177, 181

input/output, 145, 165–171

    devices, 145

    hardware, 145

Insert Object, 118

instruments (musical), 125

International applet (Control Panel), 166, 169

I/O. *See* input/output

IO.SYS, 18

ISO's Latin1 character set, 57, 60

J

jaggies, 58

K

kernel services, 93

Keyboard applet (Control Panel), 169

keyboard driver, 166, 169

KEYBOARD.DRV, 154

keyboard-specific translation table, 166

L

language-specific translation table, 166

Latin1 character set, 57, 60

launching applications, 79, 81–82, 85

lines, drawing, 54

lossless vs. lossy compression, 131

low-priority messages, 148, 150

LRU (least recently used) memory page, 163

M

MAIN.CPL, 87, 90

Main group, 75

main memory, 159, 162–163

MASKPEN drawing mode, 53

MDI. *See* multiple document interface

MDIClient window, 29

megabyte, 9

memory

   architectures, 12

   how Windows and DOS use, 9–10, 12–13

   main, 159, 162–163

   virtual, 145, 159–160, 162–163

memory pages, 160, 162–163

menu bar, 36

menu resources, 33, 36

menus, 33, 36

MERGEPEN drawing mode, 53

message-based system, Windows as, 145, 147

message queue, 147–148, 150–151

messages, 147–148, 150–151

   high- vs. low-priority, 148, 150

   sent or received by controls, 44

   sent by tasks, 145

   system waiting for, 177, 181

MIDI audio, 126, 128

MIDI synthesizer, 128

minimized windows, 30–31

modal and modeless dialog boxes, 43

Mouse applet (Control Panel), 168

mouse drivers, 156, 165, 168

MOUSE.DRV, 156

multimedia, 121–141

Multimedia Extensions, 123

multiple document interface (MDI), 29

multitasking, 189–190, 192–193

N

network DDE, 110

90/10 rule, 178

Normal mode, 160

Notepad window, 30–31

O

ObjectLink format, 116

OEM character set, 57–58, 60

OLE (object linking and embedding), 100, 104, 115–119

automation, 116

clients, 116–117, 119

servers, 115, 117–119

verbs, 116, 119

organization of Windows and DOS, 5–7

outline typeface hinting, 59, 63

outline typefaces, 59, 62–63

output device drivers, 165

output devices, 145, 165

OwnerLink format, 116

P

pages, memory, 160, 162–163

paper-clip icon, 94, 97

parent window, 26

paste (copy and cut), 100, 103–104, 106–107

Paste Special, 118

PC architecture, 153

pens, 49, 52

pen styles, 52

Pentium CPU, 9, 12

Photo-Paint (CorelDRAW)

display of, 26, 28–31

toolbox, 28

PIF Editor (Windows), 184, 187

PIFs, 184, 186–187

pipelines (DDE), 109

pixels, 50

playback drivers (animation), 138, 141

points (type size), 57

power on self test (POST), 18

preemptive multitasking, 190, 193

Printer applet (Control Panel), 170

printer drivers, 166, 170–171

Printer Setup dialog box, 167

print spooler, 166, 171

Program information files. *See* PIFs

Program Item Properties dialog box, 76

Program Manager, 16, 19, 73, 75–76, 78–79

Program Manager icons, 76

Program Manager windows, 30

Protected mode, 13

Q

question-mark icon, 66

queue, message, 147–148, 150–151

quotations, library of, 100

R

RAM, 159

raster, 50

raster fonts, 61

raster graphics, 50

rasterizing, 59, 62

raster typefaces, 58, 61

Real mode, 12–13

redraw messages (screen), 148, 150

REG.DAT, 85

resources

  cursor, 65

  dialog, 43, 46

  icon, 65

  image, 39

  menu, 33, 36

S

sampling sound, 125

sans-serif typefaces, 57

SB_HSCROLL and SB_VSCROLL
  messages, 40

SB_LINEDOWN and SB_LINEUP
  messages, 41

SB_PAGEDOWN and SB_PAGEUP
  messages, 41

SB_THUMBPOSITION and
  SB_THUMBTRACK messages, 41

scan code, 166

screen redraw messages, 148, 150

scroll bars, 34, 40–41

serifs (of type characters), 57

servers

  DDE, 109–110

  OLE, 115, 117–119

software applications groups, 75

sound, 123, 125–129

sound boards, 125, 128

sound clips, 132

Standard mode, 160

starting applications, 79, 81–82, 85

StartUp group, 75, 78

status bars, 34, 38–39

storage (*see also* memory)

  disk, 163

  multimedia, 123

storage-device I/O, 165

stretch BITBLTs, 55

strokes (of type characters), 57

stroke typefaces, 58, 61

submenus, 36–37

Symbol character set, 57

synergy, 101, 103

SYSTEM.INI, 15

T

task switching, 189–190, 192–193

text file formats, 104

thrashing, 160, 163

386 CPU, 9, 12–13

386 Enhanced applet, 160, 163

timer messages, 150, 177

time slicing, 190, 193

tool bars, 33, 38–39

translation tables (keyboard), 166

TrueType typefaces, 59, 62

TTF files, 62

286 and higher CPUs, 12–13

typeface formats, 58–59

typefaces, 57–63

Type 1 typefaces, 62

type sizes, 60

U

Unicode character set, 58

USER.EXE, 154

user interface (UI), 21–69

    components of, 5–6, 33

    consistency of, 33

    how it works, 33–41

    I/O, 165

utilities (built-in), 71–97

V

VDISK, 13

vector format (typefaces), 58

verbs (in OLE operations), 116, 119

VGA.3GR, 184

video, 123, 131–132, 134–135

video adapters, 123

video capture boards, 132, 134

video clips, 123, 131–132, 134–135

video file compression, 131–132

Video for Windows (Microsoft), 123

virtual device drivers (VxDs), 184, 187

virtual–86 emulation, 13

Virtual–86 mode, 183–184, 187

virtual machines, 186, 190

virtual memory, 145, 159–160, 162–163

Virtual Memory dialog box, 160

W

warm DDE pipelines, 109

waveform audio, 125, 128

WAV files, 125–126, 128

WIN.COM, 15, 19

window classes, 26

window-management messages, 151

Windows applications, running, 175, 177–178, 180–181

windows-based Windows environment, 25–27, 44

Windows Clipboard, 103–104, 106–107, 118

Windows display, 25–31

Windows Help, 73, 93–94, 96–97

Windows old application (WINOA), 184

WINFILE.INI, 81, 84

WinHelp utility, 93–97

WIN.INI, 87, 91

WINOA386.MOD, 184

WM_MOUSEMOVE message, 68

X

XOR bitmaps, cursor and icon, 65, 68–69

XORPEN drawing mode, 53

Imagination.
Innovation. Insight.

The How It Works Series from Ziff-Davis Press

"... a magnificently seamless integration of text and graphics ..."

Larry Blasko, The Associated Press, reviewing *PC/Computing How Computers Work*

No other books bring computer technology to life like the *How It Works* series from Ziff-Davis Press. Lavish, full-color illustrations and lucid text from some of the world's top computer commentators make *How It Works* books an exciting way to explore the inner workings of PC technology.

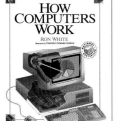

PC/Computing How Computers Work

A worldwide blockbuster that hit the general trade bestseller lists! *PC/Computing* magazine executive editor Ron White dismantles the PC and reveals what really makes it tick.

ISBN: 094-7 Price: $22.95

How Networks Work

Two of the most respected names in connectivity showcase the PC network, illustrating and explaining how each component does its magic and how they all fit together.

ISBN: 129-3 Price: $24.95

How Macs Work

A fun and fascinating voyage to the heart of the Macintosh! Two noted *MacUser* contributors cover the spectrum of Macintosh operations from startup to shutdown.

How Software Works

This dazzlingly illustrated volume from Ron White peeks inside the PC to show in full-color how software breathes life into the PC. Covers Windows™ and all major software categories.

ISBN: 133-1 Price: $24.95

How to Use Your Computer

Conquer computerphobia and see how this intricate machine truly makes life easier. Dozens of full-color graphics showcase the components of the PC and explain how to interact with them.

All About Computers

This one-of-a-kind visual guide for kids features numerous full-color illustrations and photos on every page, combined with dozens of interactive projects that reinforce computer basics, making this an exciting way to learn all about the world of computers.

How To Use Word

Make Word 6.0 for Windows Work for You!

A uniquely visual approach puts the basics of Microsoft's latest Windows-based word processor right before the reader's eyes. Colorful examples invite them to begin producing a variety of documents, quickly and easily. Truly innovative!

ISBN: 184-6 Price: $17.95

How To Use Excel

Make Excel 5.0 for Windows Work for You!

Covering the latest version of Excel, this visually impressive resource guides beginners to spreadsheet fluency through a full-color graphical approach that makes powerful techniques seem plain as day. Hands-on "Try It" sections give new users a chance to sharpen newfound skills.

ISBN: 155-2 Price: $22.95

ISBN: 166-8 Price: $15.95

ISBN: 146-3 Price: $24.95

ISBN: 185-4 Price: $17.95

Available at all fine bookstores or by calling 1-800-688-0448, ext. 100. Call for more information on the Instructor's Supplement, including transparencies for each book in the *How It Works* Series.

© 1993 Ziff-Davis Press

Fight Instant Obsolescence

- Covers the full gamut of inexpensive upgrade solutions for memory, storage, video, printers, telecommunications, and much more
- Contains "What to Look for When You Shop" information sheets that summarize features to look for and questions to ask when you are ready to make an upgrade purchase
- For anyone who wants more from their PC

CONTAINS 1 DISK

This Old PC

Dale Lewallen

Retail Price: $29.95   ISBN: 1-56276-108-0

Is your computer wilting under the memory demands of Windows? These days some PCs are practically obsolete by the time you get them home! The good news is best-selling author Dale Lewallen is here to show you how to turn that aging workhorse of a PC into a blazingly fast racehorse, eager to run today's high-performance software and peripherals. In *This Old PC* you'll learn step-by-step how easy and inexpensive it can be to upgrade your system for years of added performance. Plus you'll get a disk that contains programs to tell you what's inside your computer and utilities for upgrading your system through software. To ensure you have all the necessary facts to make an upgrade purchase, "How to Buy" information sheets that summarize features to look for and questions to ask at the store are also included.

Available at all fine bookstores, or by calling 1-800-688-0448, ext. 109.

ZIFF-DAVIS ZD PRESS

ATTENTION TEACHERS AND TRAINERS
Now You Can Teach From These Books!

ZD Press now offers instructors and trainers
the materials they need to use these books in their classes.

- An Instructor's Manual features flexible lessons designed for use in a 10- or 15-week course (30-45 course hours).

- Student exercises and tests on floppy disk provide you with an easy way to tailor and/or duplicate tests as you need them.

- A Transparency Package contains all the graphics from the book, each on a single, full-color transparency.

- Spanish edition of *PC/Computing How Computers Work* will be available.

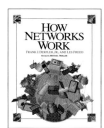   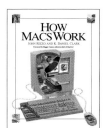

These materials are available only to qualified accounts. For more information contact:

Corporations, Government Agencies: Cindy Johnson, 800-488-8741, ext. 108

In the U.S.A: Academic Institutions: Suzanne Anthony, 800-786-6541, ext. 108

In Canada: Copp Clark Pitman Ltd.

In the U.K.: The Computer Bookshops

In Australia: WoodLane Pty. Ltd.

ZIFF-DAVIS
ZD
PRESS

Cut Here

Cut Here

Ziff-Davis Press Survey of Readers

Please help us in our effort to produce the best books on personal computing.
For your assistance, we would be pleased to send you a FREE catalog
featuring the complete line of Ziff-Davis Press books.

1. How did you first learn about this book?

Recommended by a friend . . . . ☐ -1 (5)

Recommended by store personnel . . . . ☐ -2

Saw in Ziff-Davis Press catalog . . . . ☐ -3

Received advertisement in the mail . . . . ☐ -4

Saw the book on bookshelf at store . . . . ☐ -5

Read book review in: _____ ☐ -6

Saw an advertisement in: _____ ☐ -7

Other (Please specify): _____ ☐ -8

2. Which THREE of the following factors most influenced your decision to purchase this book? (Please check up to THREE.)

Front or back cover information on book . . . ☐ -1 (6)

Logo of magazine affiliated with book . . . . . . ☐ -2

Special approach to the content . . . . ☐ -3

Completeness of content . . . . ☐ -4

Author's reputation. ☐ -5

Publisher's reputation . . . . ☐ -6

Book cover design or layout . . . . ☐ -7

Index or table of contents of book . . . . ☐ -8

Price of book . . . . ☐ -9

Special effects, graphics, illustrations . . . . . . ☐ -0

Other (Please specify): _____ ☐ -x

3. How many computer books have you purchased in the last six months? _____ (7-10)

4. On a scale of 1 to 5, where 5 is excellent, 4 is above average, 3 is average, 2 is below average, and 1 is poor, please rate each of the following aspects of this book below. (Please circle your answer.)

Depth/completeness of coverage	5	4	3	2	1	(11)
Organization of material	5	4	3	2	1	(12)
Ease of finding topic	5	4	3	2	1	(13)
Special features/time saving tips	5	4	3	2	1	(14)
Appropriate level of writing	5	4	3	2	1	(15)
Usefulness of table of contents	5	4	3	2	1	(16)
Usefulness of index	5	4	3	2	1	(17)
Usefulness of accompanying disk	5	4	3	2	1	(18)
Usefulness of illustrations/graphics	5	4	3	2	1	(19)
Cover design and attractiveness	5	4	3	2	1	(20)
Overall design and layout of book	5	4	3	2	1	(21)
Overall satisfaction with book	5	4	3	2	1	(22)

5. Which of the following computer publications do you read regularly; that is, 3 out of 4 issues?

Byte . . . . ☐ -1 (23)

Computer Shopper . . . . ☐ -2

Corporate Computing . . . . ☐ -3

Dr. Dobb's Journal . . . . ☐ -4

LAN Magazine . . . . ☐ -5

MacWEEK . . . . ☐ -6

MacUser . . . . ☐ -7

PC Computing . . . . ☐ -8

PC Magazine . . . . ☐ -9

PC WEEK . . . . ☐ -0

Windows Sources . . . . ☐ -x

Other (Please specify): _____ ☐ -y

Please turn page.

PLEASE TAPE HERE ONLY—DO NOT STAPLE

6. What is your level of experience with personal computers? With the subject of this book?

	With PCs	With subject of book
Beginner	☐ -1 (24)	☐ -1 (25)
Intermediate	☐ -2	☐ -2
Advanced	☐ -3	☐ -3

7. Which of the following best describes your job title?

Officer (CEO/President/VP/owner)........ ☐ -1 (26)
Director/head........................ ☐ -2
Manager/supervisor................... ☐ -3
Administration/staff.................. ☐ -4
Teacher/educator/trainer.............. ☐ -5
Lawyer/doctor/medical professional....... ☐ -6
Engineer/technician................... ☐ -7
Consultant.......................... ☐ -8
Not employed/student/retired........... ☐ -9
Other (Please specify): _____ ☐ -0

8. What is your age?

Under 20........................... ☐ -1 (27)
21-29............................. ☐ -2
30-39............................. ☐ -3
40-49............................. ☐ -4
50-59............................. ☐ -5
60 or over......................... ☐ -6

9. Are you:

Male............................. ☐ -1 (28)
Female............................ ☐ -2

Thank you for your assistance with this important information! Please write your address below to receive our free catalog.

Name: _____

Address: _____

City/State/Zip: _____

Fold here to mail.

1935-08-08

_____

_____

_____

BUSINESS REPLY MAIL
FIRST CLASS MAIL   PERMIT NO. 1612   OAKLAND, CA

POSTAGE WILL BE PAID BY ADDRESSEE

Ziff-Davis Press
ZIFF-DAVIS ZD PRESS
5903 Christie Avenue
Emeryville, CA 94608-1925
Attn: Marketing

NO POSTAGE
NECESSARY
IF MAILED IN
THE UNITED
STATES

Cut Here
Cut Here